Practical Guide to the Operational Use of the M240/MAG58 Machine Gun

By Erik Lawrence

Copyright ©2014 Erik Lawrence

Erik Lawrence
www.vig-sec.com   erik@vig-sec.com

Printed and bound in the United States of America

First printing 2008
Second Printing 2014

ISBN-10: 1-941998-37-2
ISBN-13: 978-1-941998-37-3
EBOOK – ISBN-13: 978-1-941998-38-0
LCCN: Not yet assigned

ATTENTION US MILITARY UNITS, US GOVERNMENT AGENCIES AND PROFESSIONAL ORGANIZATIONS: Quantity discounts are available on bulk purchases of this book. Special books or book excerpts can also be created to fit specific needs. For information, please contact:

Erik Lawrence
www.vig-sec.com   erik@vig-sec.com

Firearms are potentially dangerous and must be handled responsibly by individuals. The technical information presented in this manual reflects the author's research, beliefs, and experiences. The information in this book is presented for academic study only. Neither the author nor the publisher assumes any responsibility for the use or misuse of information contained in this book.

SAFETY NOTICE
Before starting an inspection, ensure the weapon is cleared. Do not manipulate the trigger system until the weapon has been cleared of all ammunition. Inspect the chamber to ensure that it is empty and no ammunition is present. Keep the weapon oriented in a safe direction when loading and handling.

AMMUNITION NOTICE - These weapons fire the 7.62x51 NATO (.308 Winchester), not the 7.62x54R (Rimmed/Russian). Firing the incorrect ammunition will damage the weapon and possibly injure the operator/assistant operator.

Training should be received from knowledgeable and experienced operators on this particular weapons system. Vigilant Security Services, LCC Training provides this training and continually perfects its instruction with up-to-date information from actual use

www.vig-sec.com

PREFACE

This manual is intended to be a reference for those involved in the use, maintenance and instruction of the featured firearm. My aim in writing these manuals is to set the record straight and dispel many of the false assumptions related to the different firearms. The early sections of the manual contain background material on the featured firearm which allows the user to gain the basic building blocks for further education. The firearms featured in these manuals have been used for decades by our allies and enemies, and will be for the foreseeable future, so why are we not experts with them? If I am fighting with the firearm or providing instruction on a firearm, I want to use and know their system better than they do.

The rationale for writing these manuals comes from the fact that there are not libraries of easily accessible references to use in developing your own training system for these firearms. Many of the old military field manuals are decades old and were incorrectly translated by someone who had no idea what the firearm could do, let alone basic firearm knowledge. We started from the ground up and developed the manuals to provide instruction in progressive steps that could be easily grasped and continually referred back to. A good grounding in the basics of firearms, safety, and instruction allows the user to use these manuals to their maximum value. A competent user will find little difficulty in interpreting and applying the information in the manual to their own training program.

The guide goes through the most fundamental parts of the firearm in detail and more advanced techniques are not covered as extensively. With this in mind the user can use these principles and adapt it as needed to their required level of instruction. The emphasis of this guide is in acquiring familiarity with the fundamentals of all firearms and learned competence rather than becoming a firearms guru.

Many of the points in these guides were developed from scratch in theatres of conflict and are continually improved and updated for each edition. I have continually used vetted points from users and professionals in the guides to continually update them to the best known practices for each particular firearm. If it is valid and relevant we will include it in the next edition.

Please note that this guide assumes some familiarity with the basic concepts in firearm safety, gun handling skills, common sense and an ability to process new information. Readers should have knowledge of the difference in calibers, countries of origin, and the knowledge of the priority of the skills needed for development.

I hope you find this work useful and remember that a manual does not replace proper training and hands on experience. Please email comments to erik@vig-sec.com, particularly if you find any errors or glaring omissions.

Erik Lawrence

Table of Contents

Section 1 1

  Operator Manual Introduction 1

    Description 1

    Background 3

    Variants 4

Section 2 10

  Maintenance 10

    Weapons Conditions 10

    Clearing the MAG58/M240 in Condition 1 10

    Clearing the MAG58/M240 in Condition 4 12

    Disassembling the MAG58/M240 15

    Cleaning, Lubrication and Preventive Maintenance for the MAG58/M240 25

    Assembling the MAG58/M240 29

    Function Check Procedures 31

Section 3 32

  Operation and Function 32

    Clearing the MAG58/M240 in Condition 4 34

    Cycle of Function 38

    Loading the MAG58/M240 Machine Gun 40

    Firing the MAG58/M240 41

    Barrel Change Procedure 45

    Sights/Zeroing the MAG58/M240 47

    Bipod Operations 52

    Tripod Operations 54

    Vehicle Mount 62

Section 4 65

  Performance Problems 65

    Malfunction and Immediate Action Procedures- 65

Appendix A - Ammunition 68

Appendix B- Ammunition Comparison 77

Appendix C- Training Courses 78

MAG58/M240

Machine Gun

Section 1

Operator Manual Introduction

The objective of this manual is to allow the reader to be able to use the MAG58/M240 and tripod mount system competently. The manual will give the reader background/specifications of the weapon; instruct on its operation, disassembly and assembly, demonstrate correct usage of tripod; detail proper firing procedure; and identify malfunction/misfire procedures. Operator-level maintenance will also be detailed to allow the reader to understand fully and become competent in the use and maintenance of the MAG58/M240 general-purpose machine gun.

Figure 1-1 Canadian troops carrying FN MAG in Afghanistan

Description
General Weapon Specifications
- Mode: Full-automatic only
- Operation: Gas
- Cartridge: 7.62x51mm NATO (.308 Winchester)
- Weight (without tripod or ammunition): 26 lbs./12.3 kg
- Overall length: 49 inches/124.5 cm
- Rate of fire: 650-950 rpm
- Range
  - Maximum - 3,725 meters

- o Combat Maximum effective - 1,100 meters
- o Grazing fire - 600 meters
- o Maximum effective range of the M240B for an area target:
  Tripod – 1,100 meters
  Bipod – 800 meters
- o Maximum effective range for a point target:
  Tripod – 800 meters
  Bipod – 600 meters

Feed

- Ammunition capacity: 50-round soft nylon box, 100-round cardboard box
- Disintegrating metal link - M13
- Direction: Left to right

Barrel

- Length: 24.7 inches/62.7 cm
- Quick changeable-type mechanism
- Muzzle velocity: 2,800 fps/853 m/s

Rates of Fire with the MAG58/M240

- Sustained rate of fire is 100 rounds per minute in bursts of 6 to 9 rounds in 4- to 5- second intervals. It is recommended to change the barrel if firing the sustained rate every 10 minutes.
- Rapid rate of fire is 200 rounds per minute in bursts of 6 to 9 rounds in 2- to 3- second intervals. It is recommended that the barrel be changed every two minutes if firing at the rapid rate.
- Cyclic rate of fire is the maximum amount of ammunition which can be expended in one minute. It is recommended that the barrel be changed every one minute interval if firing at the cyclic rate.

Action

- Locking feature is a rotary bolt.
- Full automatic from the open bolt
- The trigger type is a spur.
- Safety type is a cross bar-push selector with safe and fire settings.
- Safety location is on the left side above the trigger guard.

Background

Figure 1-2 M240B Machine Gun used by U.S. Troops in Afghanistan

The FN MAG is a gas-operated, belt-fed, air-cooled automatic weapon. It uses the long piston-stroke gas system with the gas regulator located below the barrel. The bolt is locked using a swinging shoulder that engages the cut in the floor of the receiver. The air-cooled barrel is quick-detachable, with the attached carrying handle to help handling of the hot barrel. The receiver is made from steel stampings.

The FN MAG is a machine gun manufactured by Fabrique Nationale (FN) in Belgium. It was developed in the 1950s, has been in production since 1958, and has become a widely adopted 7.62x51mm NATO-firing machine gun used by more than 20 countries. MAG stands for *Mitrailleuse d'Appui General*, translated as "general purpose machine gun" (GPMG). It has been adopted by more than 80 countries worldwide and is license-produced in the U.S., U.K., Argentina, Taiwan, India, Singapore, and Egypt.

The FN MAG derivative M240 manufactured by Fabrique Nationale's subsidiary FN Manufacturing, Inc., in Columbia, SC, was chosen by the U.S. military for different roles after large world-wide searches and competitions. It has mainly replaced the M60 in most roles, though it replaced some other machine guns in the co-axial. The MAG58 and variants are in production in Belgium and are currently exported to many nations. The MAG58 and its descendants will continue to see service throughout the world for some time.

The M240 is a belt-fed, gas-operated, air-cooled, crew-served, fixed-headspace weapon. It is compatible only with the M13 Link system, also used by many other western (especially NATO) machine-gun designs. Its functionality is demonstrated by its ability to be mounted on the M122A1 tripod, a bipod, on vehicles, or on aircraft.

It was first adopted in 1977 by the U.S. Army as a co-axial tank gun and slowly adopted for more applications in 1980s and 1990s. The M240 and M240E1 were adopted for use on vehicles, which led to further adoption more uses, especially for the U.S. Army and

U.S. Marine infantry. While possessing many of the same basic characteristics as its predecessor, the durability of the M240 system results in superior reliability when compared to the M60. The M240 actually has a more complex gas system than the M60, but can function better with lower maintenance and higher reliability, though these features come at greater cost and weight.

Chambered for the 7.62x51mm NATO cartridge, the MAG uses a locking system similar to that of the Browning Automatic Rifle and has made use of some other work by John Browning, who had worked on other earlier designs in Belgium. The downward locking bolt drives the belt-feed system, which is a similar type to that of the MG42, itself borrowing it from an earlier design. They are, however, not identical; the MAG works with the standard NATO-belt type, which was a capability not added until a 1968 redesign of the MG3, a descendant of the MG42. The MG42 also influenced the MAG's trigger mechanism

The FN MAG has proven to be extremely reliable under all conditions. In U.S. Army testing, it could fire, on average, 26,000 rounds until a failure (such as a part breaking). Mean rounds to a stoppage figures, such as a jam, were lower.

One popular feature of this weapon is that the barrels can be switched very quickly; indeed, during sustained usage, a well-trained crew can swap to a fresh barrel within about three seconds and are technically supposed to do so after every 200-round belt during sustained fire in order to prevent overheating. In practice, this change is often skipped, and the weapon can take it. During the Falklands War, for example, British Paratroopers participating in the assault on Goose Green were forced to fire over 8,000 rounds through individual barrels without significant pause or opportunity to change them, resulting in muzzles glowing white hot, but weapons still proving effective.

They are both (M60/M240) scheduled to be replaced by a lightweight machine gun (JSSAP/PMSW), which will also replace some of the M249 Squad Automatic Weapons. Among the likely candidates is another FN product, SOCOM's latest 7.62mm machine gun — the M249-derived Mk 48 Mod 0, scheduled for fielding starting in 2006 with U.S. Navy special operations units with whom it was developed.

The NATO version of the M240 is known as the **MAG 58**. The U.S.-made M240 family is produced under the same specifications as the MAG 58, enabling all M240 variants to have interchangeable/interoperable components with foreign-produced NATO-equivalent weapons, resulting in significant advantages in training, logistics support, tactical versatility, and joint operations. For example, an M240B's buttstock and bipod may be carried in a vehicle to enable the crew to convert the co-axial weapon to an infantry model in the event that they are forced to withdraw from an inoperable vehicle.

There are several variants, and the MAG58 has become a true general-purpose machine gun (GPMG). The following is a list of the variants:

Variants

MAG or MAG58

Figure 1-3 MAG58 Machine Gun

- **MAG58:** The FN MAG is a machine gun manufactured by Fabrique Nationale (FN), Belgium. It was developed in the 1950s, has been in production since 1958, and has become a widely adopted 7.62mm NATO-firing machine gun used by more than 20 countries. MAG stands for *Mitrailleuse d'Appui General*, translated as "general purpose machine gun" (GPMG), refer to Figure 1-3.

The M240, formally United States Machine Gun, 7.62mm, M240, is a family of belt-fed medium machine guns firing the 7.62×51mm NATO cartridge (w/M13 Link). It is based on the FN MAG machine gun, which is based on the Browning Automatic Rifle. The M240 has been used by the United States armed forces since the late 1970s. It is used extensively by infantry, as well as ground vehicles and aircraft.

All variants of the M240 series are fed from disintegrating belts and are capable of firing most types of 7.62mm NATO ammunition. They all share the same basic internal parts, which are also interchangeable, for the most part, with other members of the FN MAG family. There are significant differences in weight and some features among some versions for which this feature does not apply. The M240 is manufactured by the American division of FN Herstal, a Belgian company.

M240E4/M240B

Figure 1-4 M240B Machine Gun

- **M240B:** The M240B is the standard infantry medium machine gun of the U.S. Army and is the version in use by the U.S. Air Force. It comes configured for ground combat. It is almost always referred to as an "M240 Bravo" or even a "240 Bravo" verbally, but always written as M240B, refer to Figure 1-4.

The M60E4 (Mk 43 as designated by the U.S. Navy) was pitted against the (then-called) M240E4 in Army trials during the 1990s for a new infantry medium machine gun in a competition to replace the decades-old M60s. The M240E4 won and was then classified as the **M240B,** which led to 1000 existing M240s being sent to FN for an overhaul and a special kit that modified them for use on ground (such as a stock, a rail, etc). This step led to procurement contracts in the late 1990s for the all-new M240B. However, a new feature was added, a hydraulic buffer system to reduce the felt recoil as incorporated in the M60. While the M240B had been more reliable in the tests, it was a few pounds heavier than the M60E4, and there is a program underway for a new lightweight medium machine gun in the early 2000s. The Army M240 conversion of the M240B configuration should not be confused with the large numbers of M240/E1s converted to the M240G configuration for the Marine Corps.

M240C

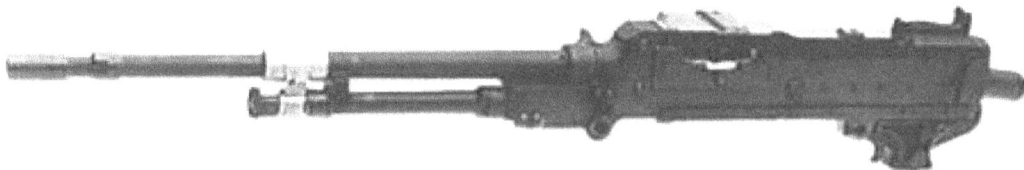

Figure 1-5 M240C Machine Gun

The M240C is the right-hand variant of the M240 that is currently used on the U.S. M2 and M3 Bradley armored fighting vehicles. The M240 C is identical to the M240 except for the ammunition feed cover and feed tray. All variants in the M240 family can be converted to right-hand feed using M240 C feeder components, refer to Figure 1-5.

M240E1 and M240D

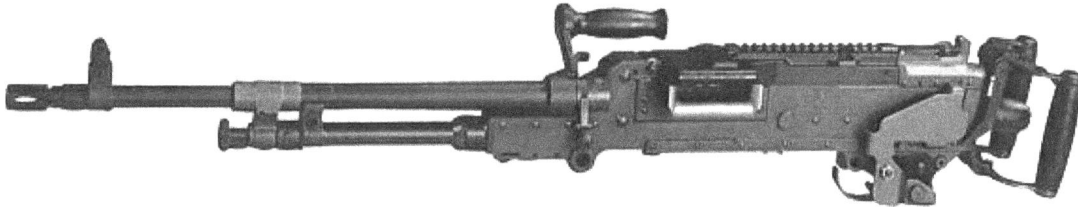

Figure 1-6 M240D Machine Gun, Left Side

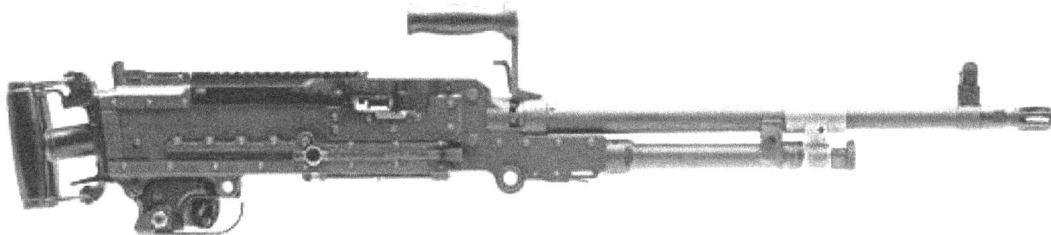

Figure 1-7 M240D Machine Gun, Right Side

The M240D has two possible configurations: aircraft and egress (ground). The aircraft-configured M240D has a front and rear sight and a trigger group which accommodates the spade grip device. The ground configuration involves the installation of an Egress Package or "infantry modification kit", which is designed to provide downed aircrew personnel with increased fire power. The M240D is an upgrade of the M240E1, primarily in the addition of an optical rail on the receiver cover. The M240E1 had also been fitted with spade grips for flexible use. FN MAG / M240D pintle-mounted machine gun of late manufacture have a Picatinny rail on the top of the receiver for the mounting of various optics and laser target designators; refer to Figures 1-6 & 1-7.

The spade-grip, pintle-mounted M240D was developed for use in military helicopters. Its smooth swing, neutral balance, and shorter length make it ideal for vehicle and naval-craft mounts. An optional egress kit enables the use of the co-axial or pintle-mounted M240 as a ground-role machine gun for self-defense by dismounted vehicle crew members. It consists of the buttstock, trigger mechanism, and bipod. It was developed in response to the need for a pintle-mount variant and has a top-mounted M1913 optical rail and other features to further improve the adaptability and utility of the M240 system.

M240G

Figure 1-8 M240G Machine Gun

A similar version of the M240, the M240G is the standard U.S. Marine Corps medium machine gun. The Marine Corps has replaced the M60E3 with the M240G. The M240 allows for commonality throughout the Marine Corps, whether the weapon is used in an infantry, vehicular, or airborne role. The M240G is the ground version of the original M240 or M240E1, 7.62mm medium class weapon designed as a co-axial/pintle- mounted machine gun for Tanks and LAVs. The M240G can be modified for ground use by the installation of an "infantry modification kit," (a flash suppressor, front sight, carrying handle for the barrel, a buttstock, infantry-length pistol grip, bipod, and rear- sight assembly). The 240G lacks a front heat guard and is few pounds lighter at 25.6 pounds than the M240B, refer to Figure 1-8.

M240E5/M240H

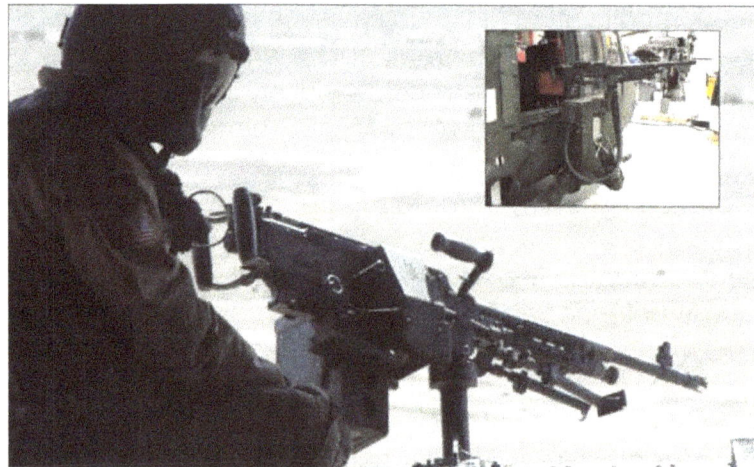

Figure 1-9 M240H Machine Gun

An improvement of the M240D, the M240H (sometimes referred to as the "240 Hotel") features a rail-equipped feed cover, an improved flash suppressor, and a configuration so that it can be more quickly converted to infantry standard using an egress kit, refer to Figure 1-9. This aviation model is designed for aviation application and demonstrates reliability equal to the M240B. It delivers two minutes of continuous suppressive fire and is removable/employable in a ground role.

M240E6

Figure 1-10 M240E6 Machine Gun, Prototype

The E6, currently in testing, is a lighter-weight model that features a titanium receiver block, refer to Figure 1-10.

Mk 48 Mod 0

Figure 1-11 Mk 48 Mod 0 Machine Gun

Mk 48 Mod 0 is a lightweight machine gun firing the 7.62×51mm NATO cartridge. It is manufactured by Fabrique Nationale Manufacturing, Inc., a division of FN Herstal based in the United States. The Mk 48 has been developed in conjunction with the U.S. Special Operations Command (USSOCOM), which has recently adopted the weapon and started its fielding process, starting with special operations units, refer to Figure 1-11.

Section 2

Maintenance

Safety Rules- The following safety rules apply at all times to all weapons.

1. Treat every weapon as if it were loaded.
2. Never point a weapon at anything you do not intend to shoot.
3. Keep your finger straight and off the trigger until you are ready to fire.
4. Keep the weapon on "SAFE" until you are ready to fire.

Weapons Conditions

Condition 1- Bolt locked to the rear. Safety ON. Ammo on the feed tray. Cover closed.

Condition 2- N/A

Condition 3- Bolt forward. Chamber empty. Safety is off. Ammo on the feed tray. Cover closed.

Condition 4- Bolt forward. Chamber empty. Safety is off. Feed tray is clear of ammo. Cover closed.

Safety

The paramount consideration while training with the machine gun is safety. It is imperative that the weapon be cleared properly before disassembly and inspection.

Clearing the MAG58/M240 in Condition 1

Weapon Condition 1: An ammunition belt is protruding from the left side; bolt is to the rear and safety on "SAFE".

Figure 2-1 Selector in the "SAFE" position

1. To clear the loaded MAG58/M240, the weapon's selector must be in the "SAFE" position (Figure 2-1).

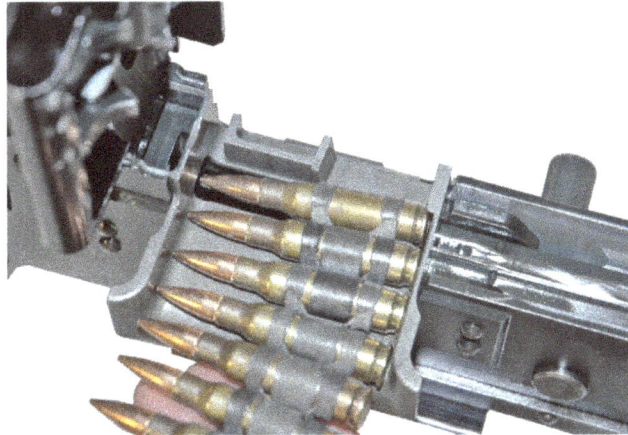

Figure 2-2 Raising the receiver cover

2. Raise the receiver cover to the fully open position. Once the receiver cover is fully opened, remove the ammunition belt link from the feed tray (Figure 2-2).

Figure 2-3 Raising the feed-tray

3. Lift the ammunition feed tray to inspect the chamber to ensure no cartridge is present (Figure 2-3).

Figure 2-4 Closing feed tray and feed tray cover

4. Close the feed tray and the feed-tray cover. Orient the weapon in a safe direction; place weapon on F"IRE" and pull the cocking handle back and ride the bolt forward

by the cocking handle. Replace the weapon's selector into the "SAFE" position (Figure 2-4).

Clearing the MAG58/M240 in Condition 4

Weapon condition 4: No ammunition belt is protruding from the right side.

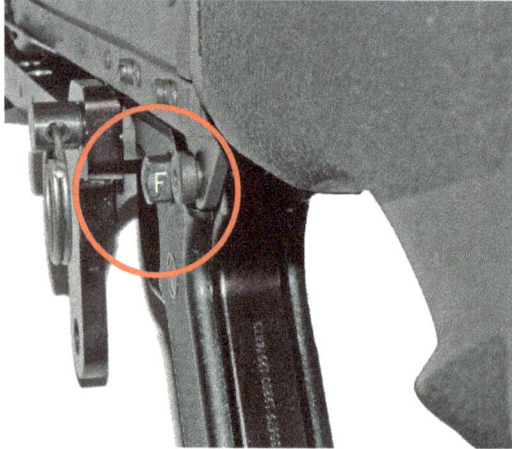

Figure 2-5 Selector in the "FIRE" position

1. To clear the MAG58/M240, ensure the weapon's selector is push to the left onto **"FIRE"** (Figure 2-5).

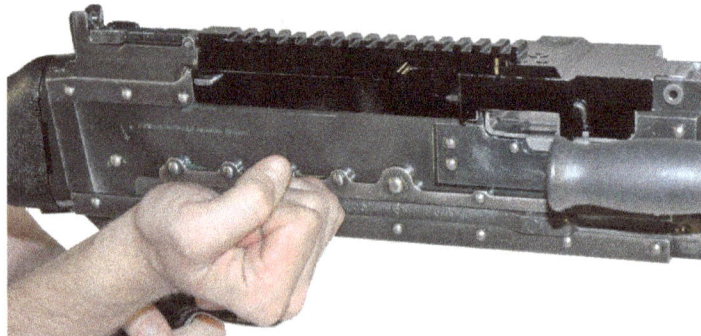

Figure 2-6 Pulling the cocking handle to the rear

2. With the right hand, (palm up) pull the cocking handle to the rear, ensuring the bolt is locked to the rear and return if forward (Figure 2-6).

Figure 2-7 Selector in the "SAFE" position

3. Place the safety on safe "**SAFE**" button pushed to the right (Figure 2-7).

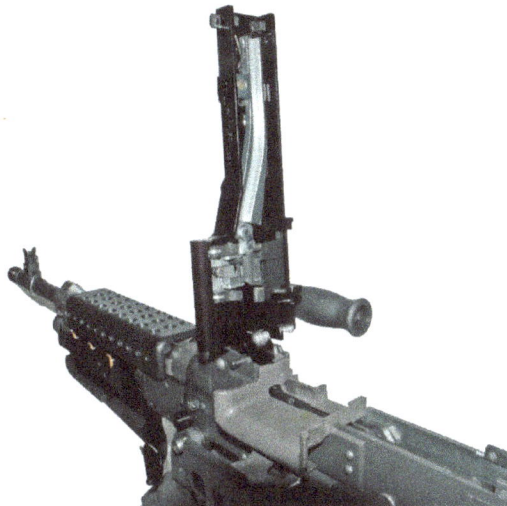

Figure 2-8 Raising the receiver cover

4. Raise the receiver cover to the fully open position and observe for live ammunition (Figure 2-8).

Figure 2-9 Raising the feed tray

5. Lift the ammunition feed tray to inspect the chamber to ensure no cartridge is present (Figure 2-9).

Figure 2-10 Riding the bolt forward

6. Close the feed tray and cover assembly and place the safety to the "FIRE" position. Pull cocking handle to the rear, and pull the trigger while manually riding the bolt forward (Figure 2-10). Close the ejection port cover (Figure 2-11).

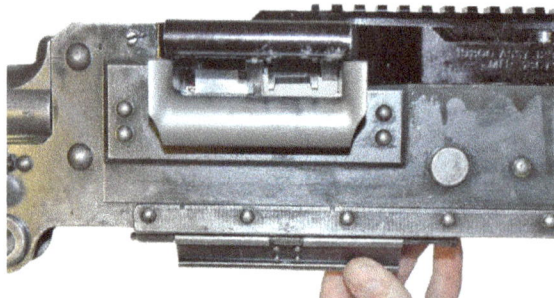

Figure 2-11 Closing the ejection port

Disassembling the MAG58/M240

To insure the proper function of the MAG58/M240, it is necessary to disassemble the weapon to inspect and clean the internal components. The names of the parts should be learned through practice in disassembling and reassembling to enhance operator competence. Generally, the parts are named for the functions they perform, i.e., the trigger guard guards the trigger, the cocking handle is used to charge the weapon, etc.

The operator performs general disassembly, which is removing and replacing the eight major groups. Disassembly beyond what is explained in this manual is detailed in the armorer version of this weapon system. During general disassembly, the operator clears the weapon. He ensures the bolt is forward before disassembly, and he places each part on a clean, flat surface, such as a table or mat. This step aids in assembly in reverse order and avoids the loss of parts.

Clear the weapon as per the above description, depending on the weapon's condition.

When the operator begins to disassemble the weapon it should be done in the following order:

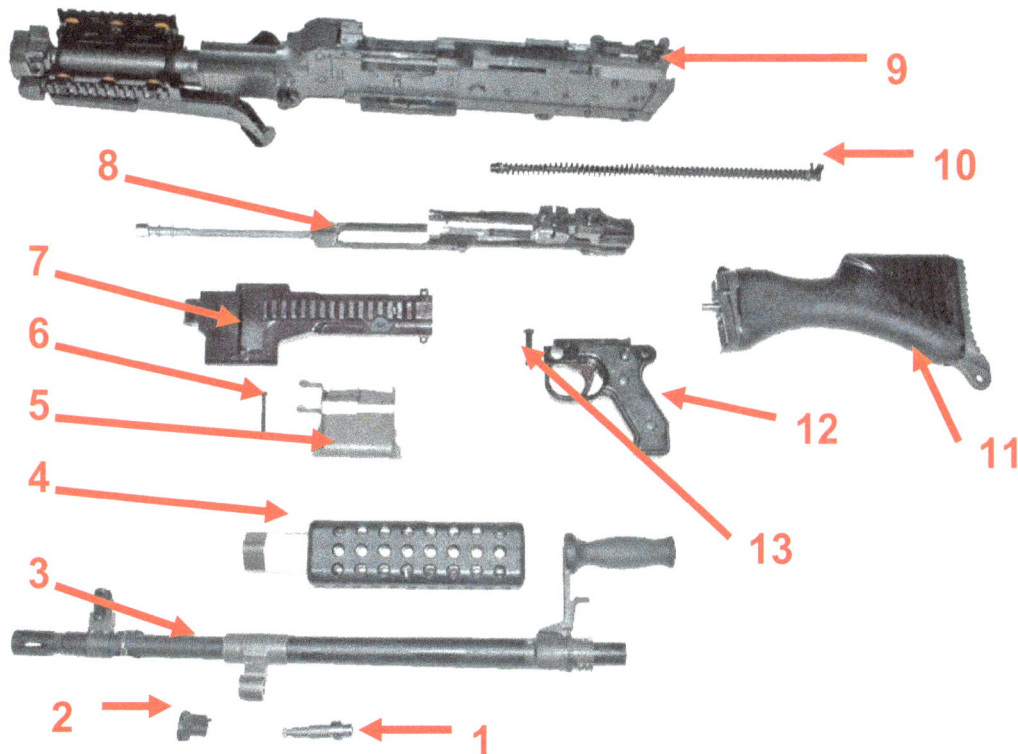

Figure 2-12 Disassembled MAG58/M240

1 – Gas Regulator Plug
2 – Gas Collar
3 – Barrel

8 – Bolt Carrier, Operating Rod and Gas Piston
9 – Receiver
10 – Driving Rod Spring Assembly

4 – Heat Shield   11 – Buttstock
5 – Feed Tray   12 – Trigger Group
6 – Cover Assembly Spring Pin   13 – Trigger Group Spring Pin
7 – Feed Tray Cover

1. Place the weapon on a flat, clean surface with the muzzle oriented in a safe direction on the extended bipod legs or tripod.

2.

Figure 2-13 Removal of buttstock

3. **Remove the Buttstock and Buffer Assembly**- Depress the back-plate latch located on the underside of the buttstock where it joins the receiver. Slide the buttstock upward (straight up) and remove it from the receiver (Figure 2-13).

DANGER- BE SURE THE BOLT IS IN THE FORWARD POSITION BEFORE DISASSEMBLY. THE SPRING GUIDE CAN CAUSE DEATH OR INJURY IF THE OPERATING ROD SPRING IS RETRACTED WITH THE BOLT PULLED TO THE REAR.

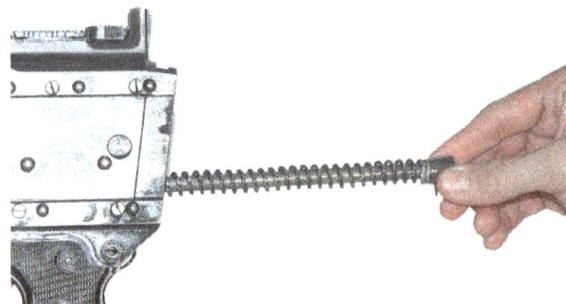

Figure 2-14a   **Figure 2-14b**
Removal of driving spring rod assembly

3. **Remove the Driving Spring Rod Assembly**- Push the driving spring rod assembly forward and up to disengage its retaining stud from inside the receiver (Figure 2-14a). Pull rearward on the drive spring rod assembly, removing it from the receiver (Figure 2-14b).

Figure 2-15 Bolt assembly removal

4. **Remove the Bolt and Operating Rod Assembly**- Pull the cocking handle to the rear to start the rearward movement of the bolt and operating rod assembly inside the receiver. With the index finger, reach inside the top of the receiver and push rearward on the face of the bolt until the bolt and operating rod assembly are exposed at the rear of the receiver. Grasp the bolt and operating rod and remove them from the rear of the receiver. Return the cocking handle to the forward position (Figure 2-15).

NOTE: Pulling the trigger maybe necessary to lower the sear and allow the bolt to release.

WARNING- To avoid injury, keep face away from rear of receiver. Hold rod assembly securely as it is under tension.

Figure 2-16 Trigger housing spring pin

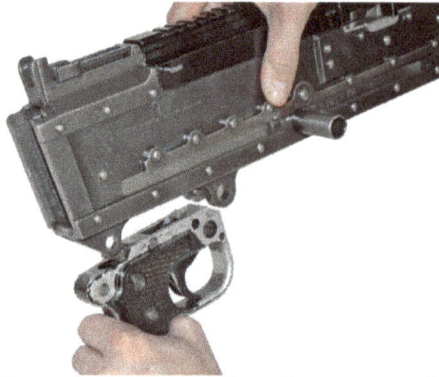

Figure 2-17 Trigger housing removal

5. **Remove the Trigger Housing Assembly**- Depress spring pin and remove. You may need to use the back of the back plate of the buttstock to tap on the spring pin, and then remove the pin with fingers (Figure 2-16). **All pins go from right to left.** Rotate the rear of the trigger-housing group assembly down, disengage the holding notch at the front of the assembly from its recess on the bottom of the receiver, and remove the assembly from the receiver (Figure 2-17).

WARNING- **When buttstock is off, do not pull the cocking handle to the rear without first removing the drive spring assembly.**

Figure 2-18a

Figure 2-18b

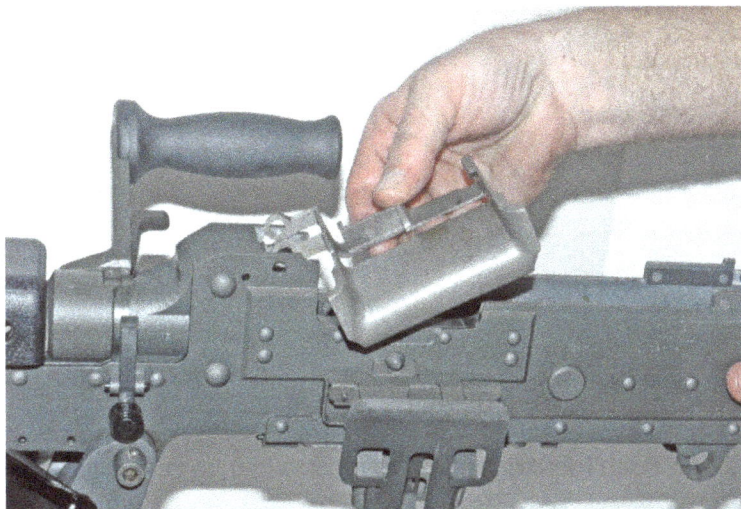

Figure 2-18c Removal of cover, feed tray, and spring pin

6. **Remove the Cover Assembly**- Close the cover. Depress the spring pin and remove. You may need to use the back of the back plate of the buttstock to tap on the spring pin. Then remove the pin with fingers. **All pins go from right to left**. Depress cover latches, lift upwards, and remove cover assembly. Remove feed tray (Figures 2-18a, b, & c).

Figure 2-19a Carrying handle to right of weapon and depress barrel-locking latch

Figure 2-19b Rotate the carrying handle to the upright position (do not lift up on the barrel release)

Figure 2-19c Push forward and up to remove the barrel from the receiver

7. **Remove the Barrel Assembly**- (A) Make sure that the barrel-carrying handle is to the right side. Depress the barrel-locking latch located on the left side of the receiver where the barrel joins the receiver and hold. (B) Grasp the barrel-carrying handle and rotate the carrying handle to the upright position (without pulling up on the barrel release). (C) Then push forward and pull up, separating the barrel from the receiver (Figures 2-19a, b, & c).

Hold barrel and twist the gas collar left

Figure 2-20a To remove the gas collar

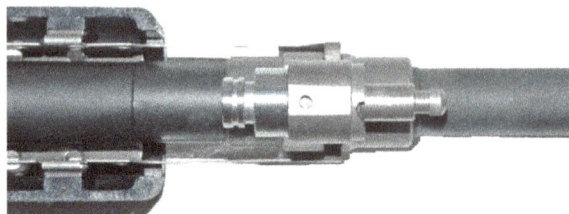

Figure 2-20b Gas collar removed

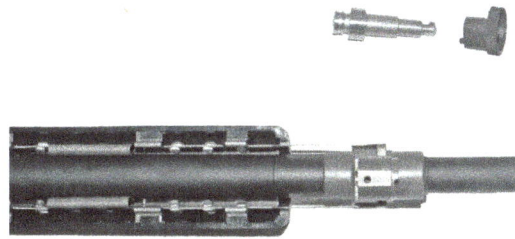

Figure 2-20c Remove the gas regulator

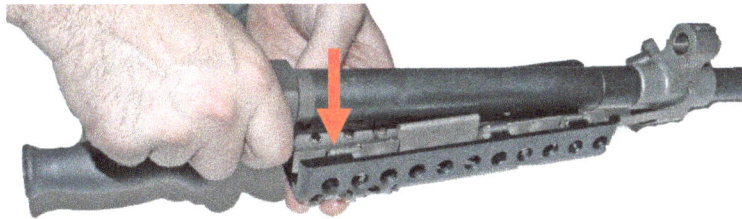

Figure 2-20d Remove the heat shield

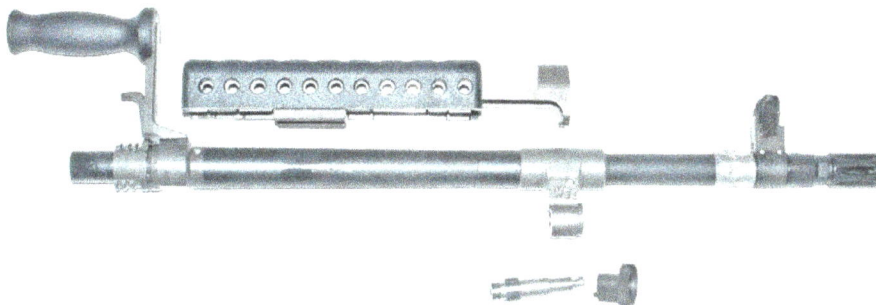

Figure 2-20e Disassembled barrel group

8. **Disassemble the Barrel Assembly.** (A) Hold the barrel at the point where the gas system attaches to it. (B) Grasp and rotate the gas collar clockwise until it releases from the gas plug. Remove the collar from the gas plug. (C) Slide the gas-regulator plug from front to rear, removing it from the gas-hole bushing. (D) Remove the heat shield. Lift the rear of the heat shield assembly off the barrel; then pry one of the front metal tabs out of the hole on the gas-hole bushing, rotate the heat shield towards the other metal tab, and remove the heat shield from the barrel. This sequence completes the general disassembly (Figure 2-20a, b, c, & d).

Inspecting the MAG58/M240

To insure a MAG58/M240 is serviceable and ready for action, it needs to be inspected periodically and between firings. This inspection can take place while the gun team is cleaning the weapon. Disassemble as per the previous section and organize the parts in groups to be inspected. Inspection begins with the weapon disassembled into its eight major assemblies. Note that a shiny surface on a part does not mean the parts are unserviceable. The operator inspects each area of the weapon and related equipment for the conditions indicated. Any broken or missing parts should be repaired or replaced. If you see rust on a weapon, the preventive maintenance should be done immediately. Inspect all of the components for broken or missing parts. Inspect parts for cracks, dents, burrs excessive wear, rust, or corrosion. Inspect external surfaces for adequate finish.

1. **Barrel Assembly-** Check barrel for bulges, bends, burrs, and obstructions or pits in the chamber or bore. Disassemble, inspect, and clean the gas collar and plug. Ensure the flash suppressor is fastened securely. Inspect the front sight for damage or looseness. Inspect carrying handle assembly for bent, broken, or missing parts. Assure the heat shield is present on the barrel assembly, is not bent or broken, and does not have any missing parts.

NOTE: Some heat distortion or charring may be observed on the outer nonmetallic portion of the heat shield and is not cause for replacement. Do not apply lubricants to composite or rubber components.

2. **Buttstock and Buffer Assembly-** Check for burrs and rough edges on mating grooves and flanges. Check to be sure the back-plate latch locks the buffer assembly securely to the receiver assembly when installed. Make sure the buffer plug sticks out through the back plate and is flush or higher than the protrusion below it. Make sure there is no rattling sound when the buffer is shaken and that the plug cannot rotate by finger pressure. Inspect the butt stock for cracks. Check to make sure the back plate locks the butt stock securely to the receiver assembly when installed.

3. **Driving Spring Rod Assembly-** Check the spring for broken strands. Ensure the rod assembly is not bent.

4. **Bolt and Operating Rod Assembly-** Inspect entire area of the bolt and operating rod assembly for missing parts, broken or cracked areas, burrs, bends, or pits on the surface. Looking at the bolt, you can see if the firing pin is broken. The extractor should not move. The operating rod piston should have a slight movement from left to right (about 1/8-inch turn). When the bolt and operating rod are pulled to the rear, the piston should move freely without binding.

NOTE: Always turn both barrels in with the weapon if damage is found on the bolt assembly.

5. **Trigger Mechanism/Housing Assembly-** Inspect the tripping lever and sear for burrs on edges. Push the tripping lever back to raise the sear, put the safety on "S," and pull

the trigger. The sear should not drop down far enough to lock in the downward position. Place the safety on "F," and pull the trigger. The sear should drop down and lock in the downward position. Check the sear spring, ensuring the leg of the spring is behind the trigger pin and not between the trigger and the pin. Check grip assembly for loose or missing grip screws. Check trigger guard for bends or cracks. Check trigger spring pin for bends, and or broken or missing spring.

6. **Cover Assembly**- Pivot the feed lever back and forth to ensure it operates smoothly without binding. Push in on the cover latches to make sure the retaining clip is not weak or missing and that they do not bind in the housing. Push down on the cartridge guides and feed pawls to make sure the springs are not weak or missing. Inspect accessory mounting rail for nicks or burrs.

7. **Feed Tray**- Check for cracks, deformation, broken welds, or loose rivets.

8. **Handguard**- Check handguard for cracks and broken or missing parts.

9. **Receiver Assembly**- Check that the rear sight assembly is securely mounted to the receiver and operates properly. Check that the cocking handle operates the slide properly. Pull the cocking handle to the rear and allow it to return forward slowly, making sure that the slide does not bind in the receiver. Check for damaged or missing ejection port cover, spring, and pin. Lower and raise the bipod legs, ensuring they move freely without binding. Check bipod legs for cracks, or twisted or incomplete assembly. Check the exterior surface of the M240B for the exterior protective finish.

MAG58/M240 completely disassembled and ready for cleaning and inspection

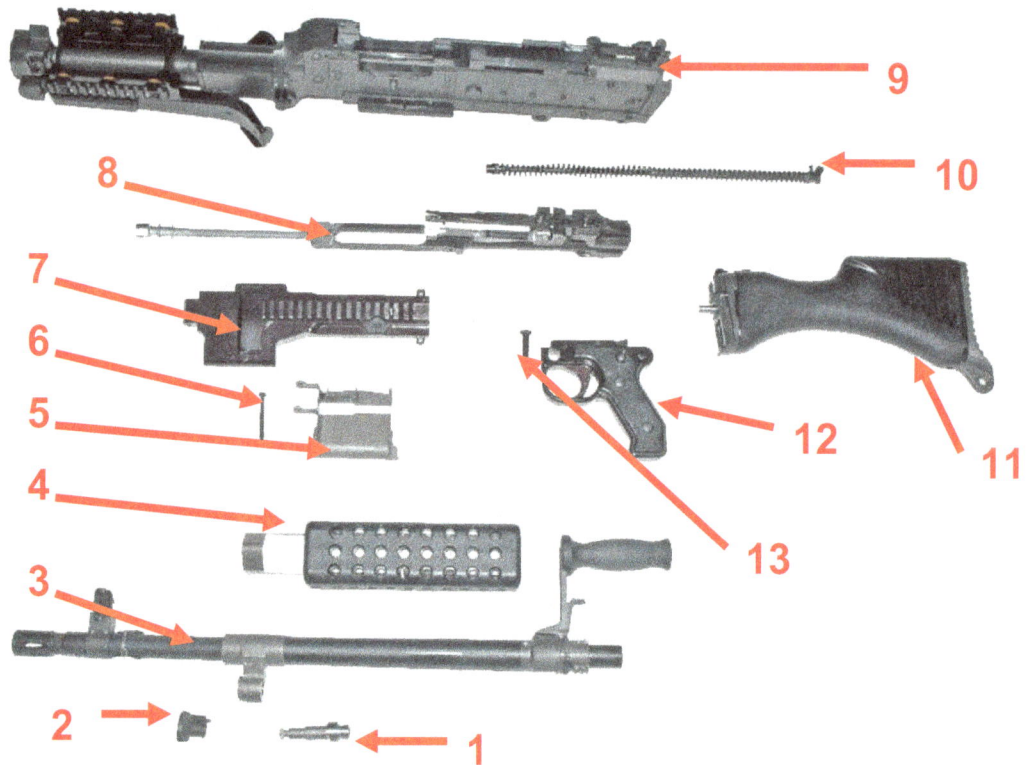

Figure 2-21 Disassembled MAG58/M240

1 – Gas Regulator Plug
2 – Gas Collar
3 – Barrel
4 – Heat Shield
5 – Feed Tray
6 – Cover Assembly Spring Pin
7 – Feed Tray Cover

8 – Bolt Carrier, Operating Rod and Gas Piston
9 – Receiver
10 – Driving Rod Spring Assembly
11 – Buttstock
12 – Trigger Group
13 – Trigger Group Spring Pin

Cleaning, Lubrication and Preventive Maintenance for the MAG58/M240

The machine gun should be cleaned immediately after firing. At a minimum, the MG should be cleaned after firing a basic load of 900 to 1,200 rounds. The operator disassembles the MG into its major groups for cleaning. All metal components and surfaces that have been exposed to powder fouling should be cleaned using CLP on a bore-cleaning patch. CLP is used on the bristles of the receiver brush to clean the receiver. After the MG is cleaned and wiped dry, a thin coat of CLP is rubbed on using a cloth. This lubricates and preserves the exposed metal parts during all normal temperature ranges.

CAUTION: When using CLP, do not use other cleaners. Never mix CLP with RBC or LSA. When cleaning the barrel, avoid getting CLP or RBC in the gas regulator. Damage could occur to the weapon.

When cleaning the weapon, any of the previously mentioned cleaning lubricating agents can be used. As soon as possible after firing the M240B, the operator disassembles the weapon into its eight major assemblies and cleans them as follows. Before the weapon is disassembled, ensure it is clear.

Clean the bore using CLP or RBC and a bore brush with a cleaning rod. Do not reverse direction of the bore brush while it is in the bore. Run the brush through the bore several times until most of the powder fouling and other foreign matter has been removed. Swab out the bore several times using a cleaning rod and a swab wet with CLP. Swab out the bore several times using a cleaning rod and a dry swab.

Clean the chamber using CLP and a chamber brush attached to a cleaning rod. Run the brush through the chamber several times until most of the powder fouling and other foreign matter has been removed. Swab out the chamber several times using a cleaning rod and a swab wet with CLP. Swab out the chamber several times using a cleaning rod and a dry swab.

Clean the receiver using a receiver brush and CLP. Brush the receiver until most of the powder fouling and other foreign matter is removed. Swab out the receiver several times using a cleaning rod section and a swab wet with CLP. Swab out the receiver several times using a cleaning rod section and a dry swab.

Clean the gas regulator plug with special tools (cleaning reamers and combination regulator scraper). Remove all carbon dust. Do not use CLP on the collar, gas block, or body. Clean each gas inlet hole of the gas regulator plug. Insert the small reamer into each hole and twist back and forth to remove the carbon (apply hand pressure only). Clean the central hole of the gas plug by inserting the scraper tool down to the bottom of the hole and twisting firmly. Clean the two grooves by inserting the scraper tool into the grooves and applying pressure as firmly as possible.

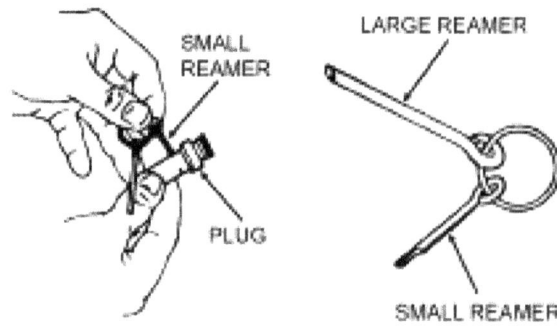

Figure 2-22 Tools for cleaning the gas regulator plug inlet holes

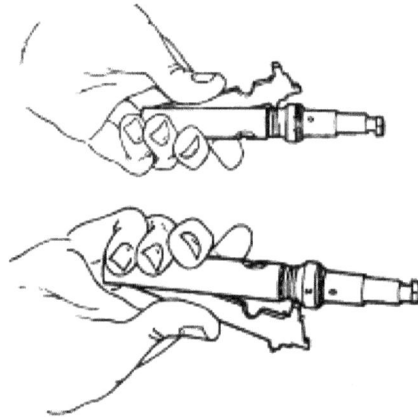

Figure 2-23 Cleaning the gas regulator plug grooves

Clean the gas cylinder with the special tool scraper-extraction combination tool, Figure 2-22. Clean the front interior of the gas cylinder by carefully inserting the combination tool, with the handle upward. Be sure the tool is fully inserted and seated against the gas cylinder, Figure 2-23. Apply slight pressure to the handles and turn clockwise to remove carbon. Clean gas cylinder bore with gas cylinder cleaning brush dampened with CLP. Brush the gas cylinder until most of the powder fouling and other foreign matter are removed.

CAUTION: When inserting the scraper-extractor combination tool into the gas cylinder, ensure before scraping that it is fully seated against the fore-end face of the cylinder. Damage to the fore-end of the gas cylinder could cause gas leakage and subsequent weapon stoppage.

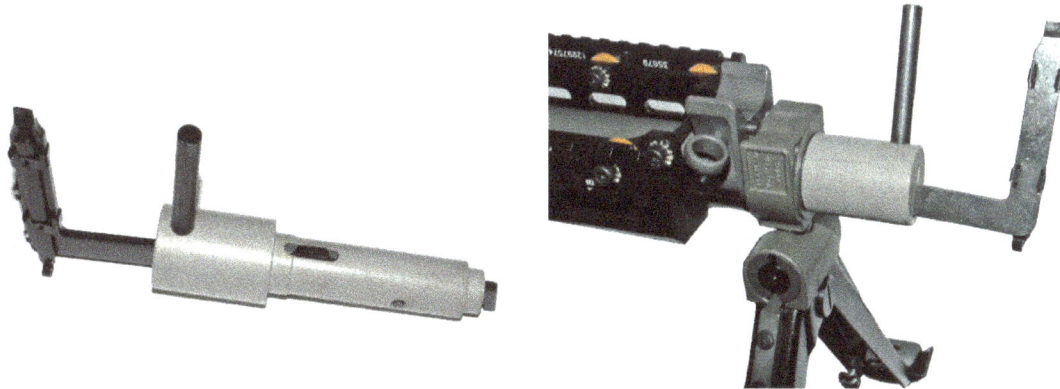

Figure 2-24a Cleaning tool for the gas cylinder   Figure 2-24b Cleaning gas cylinder with tool

Clean the bolt and operating rod with the special scraper-extraction combination tool. Clean the piston head cavity by inserting the combination tool into the piston bottom of the operating rod, Figure 2-24a &b. Squeeze the handles firmly and twist the tool to remove carbon. Insert the screwdriver end of the tool into the piston to remove carbon residue on the bottom, Figure 2-25. Clean the bolt and operating rod with rag and CLP.

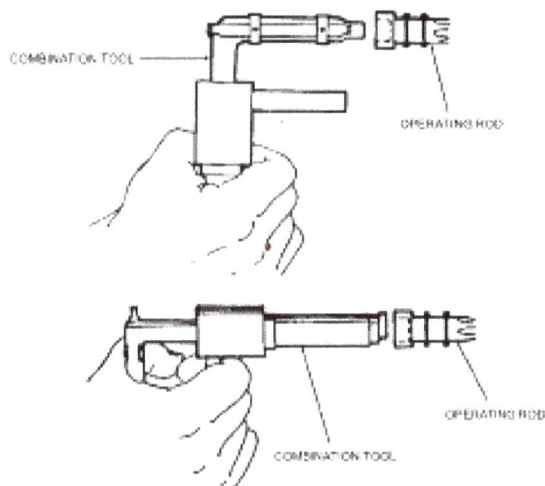

Figure 2-25 Cleaning tool for the piston head cavity

Remember the following important points during cleaning:
- Do not use gasoline, kerosene, benzene, shaving cream, high-pressure water, steam, or air for cleaning.
- Keep the gas hole bushing free of CLP or RBC. It must remain dry.
- During sustained firing, especially when using blank ammunition, the extractor assembly must be stripped and cleaned periodically.
- Improper cleaning of the gas cylinder and gas regulator plug will result in the two temporarily welding themselves together during firing.

Lubricate the following parts with CLP as instructed:
- Driving spring rod assembly.
- Bolt

- Receiver inner walls
- Cover assembly (springs, and feed pawls)
- Trigger housing (inside only)

After lubricating, the components are cycled by hand to spread the CLP. Weapons fired infrequently or stored for prolonged periods should have a light film of CLP. This should be applied to the interior of the gas cylinder and the gas piston immediately after cleaning or after inspection. Preventive maintenance is performed every 90 days, unless inspection reveals more frequent servicing is necessary. The use of the lubricant does not eliminate the requirement for cleaning and inspecting to ensure that corrosion has not formed. Before the weapon is used, the gas system and components must be cleaned and free of oil and lubricants.

All exposed surfaces of the M122A1 tripod, flex-mount assembly, complete pintle, and T&E mechanism are cleaned by wiping them down with a clean rag. For T&E and pintles that have stubborn areas with hard-to-remove dirt, a steel brush or bore brush is used to loosen the dirt (do not use on the flex-mount itself). A clean rag is then used to wipe them down, and CLP is used to lubricate them.

The following procedures apply to cleaning and lubricating the M240B during unusual conditions:
- Below 0 degrees Fahrenheit - use lubricating oil, arctic weather (LAW). Oil lightly to avoid freeze-up.
- Extreme heat - use light coat of CLP.
- Damp or salty air - use CLP. Clean and apply frequently.
- Sandy or dusty areas - use CLP. Clean and apply frequently. Wipe with rag after each application to remove excess.

Assembling the MAG58/M240

As you are assembling the MAG58/M240 machine gun, reinspect the internal parts to insure that each is in working order. After cleaning, lubricating, and inspecting the weapon, the operator assembles the weapon and performs a function check.

Figure 2-26 Replacement of the barrel assembly

1. **Replacing the Barrel Assembly**- Insert the gas regulator plug into the gas hole bushing so that it is on the number 1 setting. (Number 1 gas setting on the regulator faces towards the barrel). Place the gas collar over the front end of the gas regulator plug; while pushing against the spring, rotate counterclockwise until it stops. Insert one of the metal tabs of the heat shield into the hole located on the sides of the gas hole bushing, and then rotate it so that the other tab locks in place. Then push down on the heat shield so that it snaps onto the barrel. With gas regulator downward and carrying handle in the vertical position, place barrel on the barrel support (located on the gas cylinder). Keeping the gun upright, pull the barrel to the rear ensuring the gas regulator is guided into the gas cylinder. Pull the barrel fully into the receiver and rotate the carrying handle completely to the right, making sure to count the number of clicks. If the number of clicks falls between 2 to 7, the headspace is set correctly. If the number falls outside 2 to 7, turn it in to the unit armor (make sure that the threads on the barrel are located on the top and bottom, and on the inside of the receiver, make sure that the threads are located on the left and right) (Figure 2-26).

2. **Replacing the Cover Assembly and Feed Tray**- Position the feed tray on the receiver so that the feed tray guides are aligned with the receiver brackets. Place the cover assembly onto the receiver, aligning its mounting holes with the mounting brackets on the receiver, close the cover assembly. Then, insert the spring pin into the holes to affix the cover and feed tray to the receiver (insert the spring of the spring pin into the hole, and then push in from right to left).

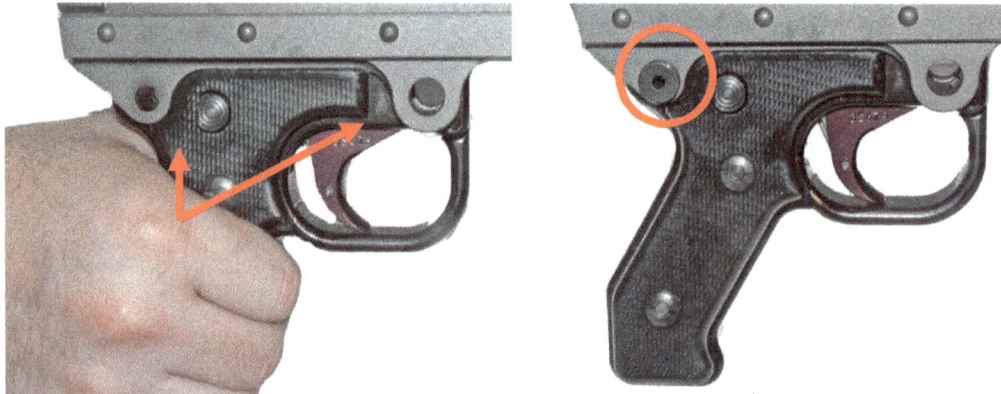

Figure 2-27 Replacement of the trigger housing assembly (forward and up and insert pin)

3. **Replacing the Trigger Housing Assembly**- Insert the holding notch on the front of the trigger housing into the forward recess on the bottom of the receiver. Rotate the rear of the trigger housing upwards and align the holes of the trigger housing with the mounting bracket on the receiver. Hold the trigger housing assembly and insert the spring pin into the hole, securing the assembly to the receiver (insert the spring of the spring pin into the hole, and then push in from right to left) (Figure 2-27).

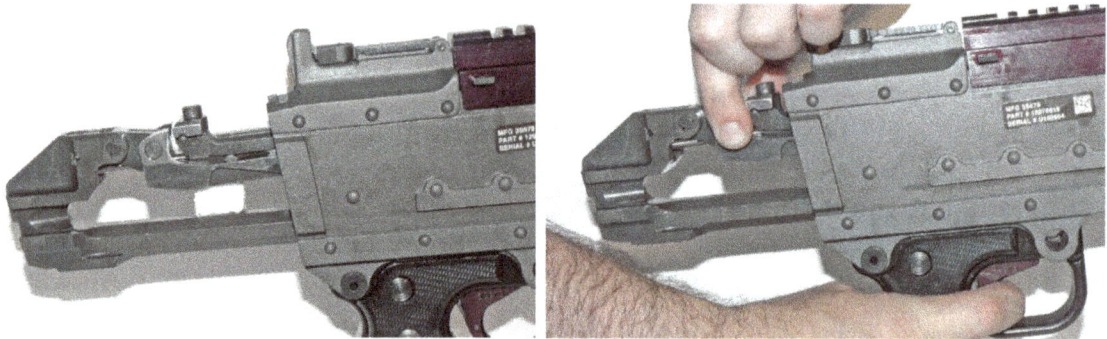

Figure 2-28 Replacement of the bolt and operating rod assembly

4. **Replacing the Bolt and Operating Rod Assembly**- Make sure the bolt and operating rod are fully extended (unlocked position). Insert the bolt and operating rod into the rear of the receiver (bolt upward, operating rod beneath bolt), ensuring the bolt is on top of the rails located on the left and right inner walls of the receiver. Push the entire bolt and operating rod assembly into the receiver as far forward as possible. Pull the trigger to allow the sear to drop and the group to slide all the way into the receiver (Figure 2-28).

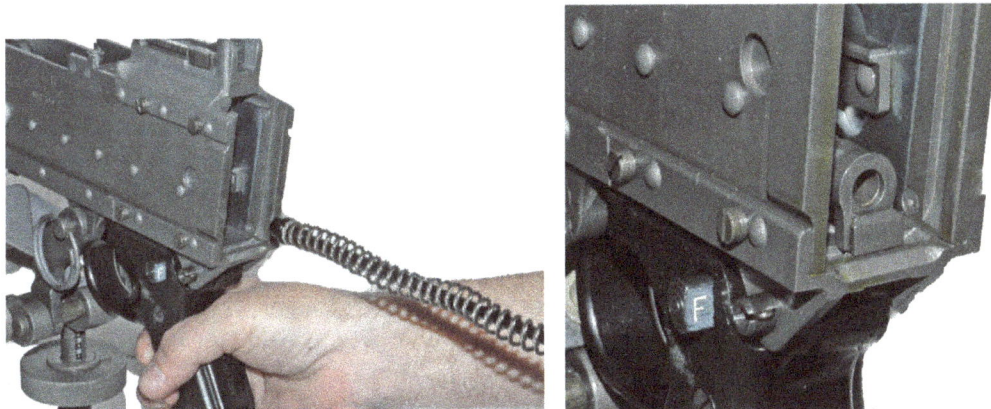

Figure 2-29 Replacement of the driving spring rod assembly

5. **Replacing the Driving Spring Rod Assembly**- Insert the driving spring rod assembly into the receiver, sliding it all the way forward against the recess in the rear of the operating rod. Push in and lower the driving spring rod assembly to engage the retaining stud into the hole located on the bottom of the receiver (Figure 2-29).

6. **Replacing the Buttstock and Buffer Assembly-** Position the bottom recess grooves of the buttstock onto the top of the receiver recess grooves. Slide the buttstock down until it locks in place on the receiver. Ensure the buttstock is secure.

7. **Replacing the Handguard**- Line up the handguard on the bottom of the gas cylinder and push upwards. The handguard snaps in place.

Function Check Procedures

1. Place the safety on "FIRE."

2. Pull the cocking handle to the rear, locking the bolt to the rear of the receiver.

3. Return the cocking handle to the forward position.

4. Place the safety on "SAFE," and close the cover.

5. Pull the trigger (bolt should not go forward).

6. Place the safety on "FIRE."

7. Pull the cocking handle to the rear, pull the trigger, and manually ride the bolt forward.

8. Close the ejection port cover.

Section 3

Operation and Function

The M240B machine gun is loaded from the closed-bolt position. The M240B is fired, unloaded, and cleared from the open-bolt position. The safety must be placed on "FIRE" before the bolt can be pulled to the rear. Before belted ammunition can be used, it must be linked with the double link at the open end of the bandoleer. It must be free of dirt and corrosion. In almost all cases, the M240B machine gun can be best used when fired from a tripod; the M240B's potential for continuous, accurate fire and control manipulation is maximized. However, in some circumstances, the operator may use the bipod mount.

Safety Rules- The following safety rules apply at all times to all weapons.

1. Treat every weapon as if it were loaded.
2. Never point a weapon at anything you do not intend to shoot.
3. Keep your finger straight and off the trigger until you are ready to fire.
4. Keep the weapon on safe until you are ready to fire.

Weapons Conditions

A. Condition 1: Ammunition is in the position on the feed tray with the cover closed. The bolt is locked to the rear and the safety is on "**SAFE**".

B. Condition 2: This weapon condition does not apply to the MAG58/M240.

C. Condition 3: Ammunition is in the position on the feed tray with the cover closed. The chamber is empty. The bolt is forward and the safety is on "**FIRE**".

D. Condition 4: The feed tray is clear of ammunition, the chamber is empty, the bolt is forward, and the safety is on "**FIRE**".

Safety

The paramount consideration while training with the machine gun is safety. It is imperative that the weapon be cleared properly before disassembly and inspection.

Clearing the MAG58/M240 in Condition 1

Weapon condition 1: An ammunition belt is protruding from the left side; bolt is to the rear and safety on "SAFE".

Figure 3-1 Selector in the "SAFE" position

1. To clear the loaded MAG58/M240, the weapon's selector must be in the "SAFE" position (Figure 3-1).

Figure 3-2 Raising the receiver cover

2. Raise the receiver cover to the fully open position. Once the receiver cover is fully opened, remove the ammunition belt link from the feed tray (Figure 3-2).

Figure 3-3 Raising the feedtray

3. Lift the ammunition feed tray to inspect the chamber to ensure no cartridge is present (Figure 3-3).

Figure 3-4 Closing feed tray and feed tray cover

4. Close the feed tray and the feed-tray cover. Orient the weapon in a safe direction; place weapon on "FIRE" and pull the cocking handle back and ride the bolt forward by the cocking handle. Replace the weapon's selector into the "SAFE" position (Figure 3-4).

Clearing the MAG58/M240 in Condition 4

Weapon condition 4: No ammunition belt is protruding from the right side.

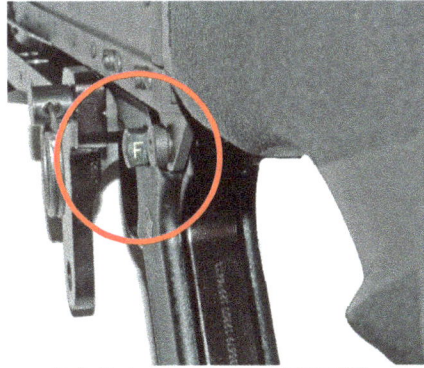

Figure 3-5 Selector in the "FIRE" position

7. To clear the MAG58/M240, ensure the weapon's selector is push to the left onto "**FIRE**" (Figure 3-5).

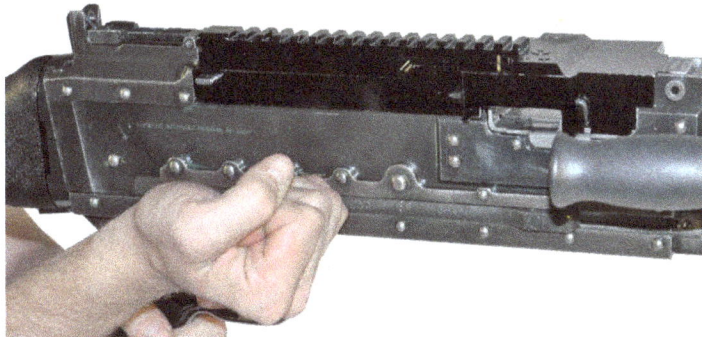

Figure 3-6 Pulling the cocking handle to the rear

8. With the right hand, (palm up) pull the cocking handle to the rear, ensuring the bolt is locked to the rear and return if forward (Figure 3-6).

Figure 3-7 Selector in the "SAFE" position

9. Place the safety to the "**SAFE**" position (button pushed to the right) (Figure 3-7).

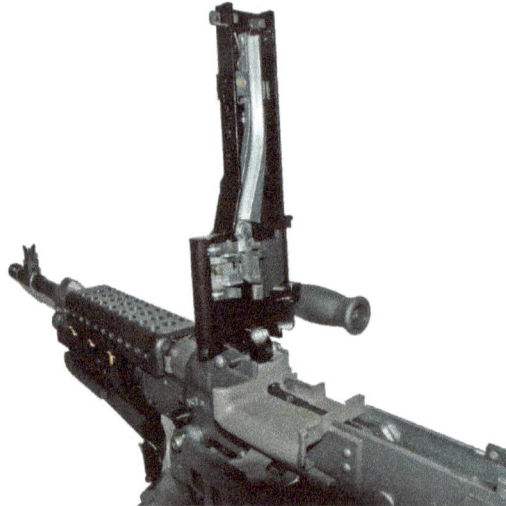

Figure 3-8 Raising the receiver cover

10. Raise the receiver cover to the fully open position and observe for live ammunition (Figure 3-8).

Figure 3-9 Raising the feedtray

11. Lift the ammunition feed tray to inspect the chamber to ensure no cartridge is present (Figure 3-9).

Figure 3-10 Riding the bolt forward

12. Close the feed tray and cover assembly and place the safety to the "FIRE" position. Pull cocking handle to the rear, and pull the trigger while manually riding the bolt forward (Figure 3-10). Close the ejection port cover (Figure 3-11).

Figure 3-11 Closing the ejection port

Cycle of Function

The operators can recognize and correct stoppages when they know how the MAG58/M240 machine gun functions. The weapon functions automatically as long as ammunition is fed into it and the trigger is held to the rear. Each time a round is fired, the parts of the weapon function in a cycle or sequence. Many of the actions occur at the same time.

These actions are separated in this manual only for instructional purposes.

Crew members can recognize and correct stoppages when they know how the weapon functions. The weapon functions automatically as long as ammunition is fed into it and the trigger is held to the rear. Each time a round is fired, the parts of the weapon function in a cycle or sequence. Many of the actions occur at the same time and are separated only for teaching purposes. The sequence of functioning is known as the "cycle of functioning."

The cycle starts when the first round of the belt is placed in the tray groove. Then the trigger is pulled, releasing the sear from the sear notch. When the trigger is pulled to the rear, the rear of the sear lowers and disengages from the sear notch, allowing the bolt and operating rod assembly to be driven forward by the expansion of the driving spring rod assembly. The cycle stops when the trigger is released and the sear again engages the sear notch on the bolt and operating rod assembly.

The details of the cycle of functioning follows:

(1) *Feeding*. The actuating roller moves the feed lever from side to side, which in turn moves the feed pawls. The forward movement of the bolt forces the outer pawls to the right, fully feeding the round. The inner pawl rides over the round and settles behind it. The rearward movement forces the inner pawl to the right, fully feeding the round. The action of fully feeding a round pushes the link of a fired round out of the side of the gun. The last link in a belt cannot be pushed out and is cleared during unloading.

(2) *Chambering*. The first round is positioned in line with the chamber and is held in position by the cartridge stop and cartridge guide pawl. On trigger squeeze, the nose of the sear is depressed, thus freeing the piston rod extension. The driving spring rod assembly pushes the working parts forward. The feed horn strikes the base of the round. The bolt strips the round from the belt link. The chambering ramp angles downward and, along with the spring tension of the cartridge guide pawl, forces the round toward the chamber. The cartridge guide pawl also holds back the belt link. When the round is fully seated in the chamber, the extractor snaps over the extractor rim of the cartridge, and the ejector is depressed.

WARNING- The M240B is carried loaded with the bolt locked to the *rear* in all *tactical situations* where noise discipline is critical to the success of the mission. Trained gun crews are the only personnel authorized to load the M240B and only

when command directs the crew to do so. During *normal training exercises*, the M240B is loaded and carried with the bolt in the *forward position*.

(3) ***Locking***. During chambering, as soon as the piston begins to move, the firing pin is withdrawn into the bolt block. The breech remains locked during the primary movement. The bolt enters the barrel breech as the operating rod is driven forward by the drive spring and as the locking lever on which the bolt is riding swings forward, pushing the bolt forward and locking it to the barrel breech. Although the term "locking" is used here, in the M240B, the bolt and barrel do not physically interlock. This way, the barrel can be removed when the bolt is forward.

(4) ***Firing***. As the working parts come forward and the round is fed into the chamber, the locking lever is forced down by the locking cams. This action slows down the forward movement of the bolt assembly. The piston rod extension, still moving forward, causes the locking lever link to rotate downward and back, forcing the arms down to their fullest extent in front of the locking shoulder. The extractor rises over the base of the round and the ejector is compressed. The round is now fully home with the breech locked. The final forward movement of the piston extension drives the firing pin through the bolt assembly onto the cartridge primer and fires the round. The working parts are now fully forward.

(5) ***Unlocking***. When the round is fired, some of the gases pass through the gas plug regulator into the gas cylinder. The rapidly expanding gases enter the hollow end cap of the gas piston and force the operating assembly to the rear, which powers the last four steps in the cycle of functioning. During the primary movement of the operating rod assembly, it moves independently of the bolt for a short distance. At this point, the locking lever begins to swing toward the rear, carrying the bolt with it into its unlocked position, and clearing the barrel breech. When the bolt assembly has been jerked back, slightly enough to unlock the breech, the primary effort is extraction of the empty case.

(6) ***Extraction***. When the breech is fully unlocked and the bolt assembly starts its rearward movement, the extractor withdraws the empty case from the chamber.

(7) ***Ejecting***. As the cartridge case is withdrawn from the chamber, the ejector pushes from the top, and the extractor pulls from the bottom. The casing falls down from the face of the bolt as soon as it reaches the cartridge-ejection port. The empty belt links are forced out the link ejection port as the rearward movement of the bolt causes the next round to be positioned in the tray groove.

(8) ***Cocking***. As the working parts continue toward the rear, the return spring is compressed, the trigger is kept squeezed, sufficient is gas made available by the gas-regulator adjustment, which causes the working parts to rebound off the buffer, and the action of feeding and firing continues. In releasing the trigger, the sear remains down, but the tripping lever rises. As the working parts come to the rear, the end of the piston rod extension hits the tripping lever, which in turn allows the sear to rise and engage the sear notch, which holds the working parts to the rear.

Loading the MAG58/M240 Machine Gun

The operator makes sure the weapon is cleared. Place the safety on "F." With your palm facing up, pull the cocking handle to the rear, which puts the bolt assembly in the rear position. When the bolt is held to the rear by the sear, manually return the cocking handle to the forward position and place the safety on "S." Raise the cover assembly and ensure the feed tray, receiver assembly, and chamber are clear. Lower the feed tray, place the safety on "F," and pull the cocking handle to the rear. While maintaining rearward pressure, pull the trigger and ease the bolt assembly forward. Place the first round of the belt in the feed-tray groove, <u>double link leading</u>, with open side of links face down Figure 3-12). Hold the belt about six rounds from the loading end while closing the cover assembly (Figure 3-13). *Ensure that the round remains in the feed tray groove, and close the cover assembly.*

Figure 3-12 Loading (first round and double link against the cartridge stop)

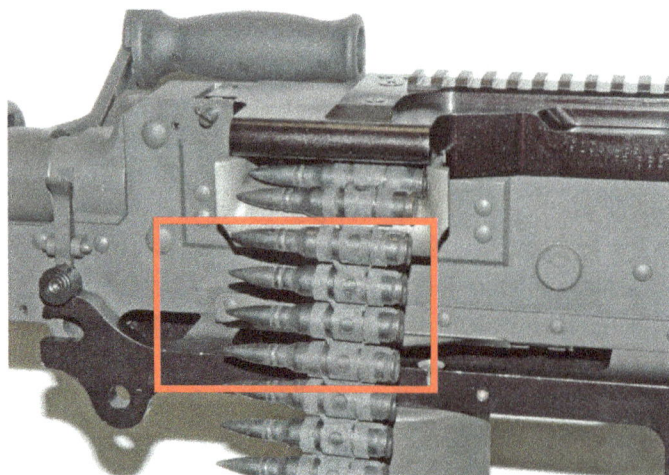

Figure 3-13 Hold the 6th-ish round while closing the cover

WARNING- The MG is carried loaded with the bolt locked to the *rear* in all *tactical situations* where noise discipline is critical to the success of the mission. Trained gun crews are the only personnel authorized to load the MG and only when command directs the crew to do so. During *normal training exercises*, the MG is loaded and carried with the bolt in the *forward position*.

Close the feed tray and cover assembly and place the safety in the "**FIRE**" position. Pull the cocking handle to the rear, and pull the trigger while manually riding the bolt forward. Close the ejection port cover.

Another loading alternative exists when the weapon is not to be used immediately but can be quickly put into action. Have the bolt forward, feed-tray cover closed and locked, and safety selector on "**SAFE**". Push the exposed double ling (brass down) or starter tab until the first round is engaged by the feed pawl.

When you need to load and fire, place the weapon on fire, pull the charging handle to the rear, and return it forward.

Pull the trigger to release the bolt to go forward, repeat the charging sequence, and fire the weapon.

NOTE: This method can also be used as an alternative to opening the feed-tray cover to reload a weapon that has completely fired the belt that was in the weapon. This procedure is how the M2 BMG and Mk 19 are loaded, the double cycle.

Unloading the MAG58/M240

The operator unloads the M240B by pulling and locking the bolt to the rear position, if it is not already there. Manually return the cocking handle to its forward position. Place the safety on "S." Raise the cover assembly and remove any ammunition or links from the feed tray. Perform the four-point safety check

Firing the MAG58/M240

Orient toward the desired area/target, take a proper sight alignment and sight picture, press the safety to the "FIRE" position, and pull the trigger. You would maintain a 6- to 9-round burst for control and avoid the overheating of the barrel when possible. Firing more than 200 rounds continuously will increase the possibility of cook offs (the heat of the barrel is so great that it ignites the powder in the unchambered round).

Figure 3-14 Selector in "SAFE" position

Once your target engagement is complete, push the safety to the left "SAFE" position. (Figure 3-14).

ENGAGE TARGETS. To engage targets effectively, you will need to know how to employ the gun using the tripod, bipod, and proper body position.

The MAG58/M240 can be fired utilizing either the attached bipod mount or by mounting the MAG58/M240 on the tripod. The tripod provides the most stable base for the weapon, enabling the operator to maximize its range capabilities and deliver a high degree of accurate fire on target.

The traversing and elevating (T&E) mechanism permits controlled manipulation in both direction and elevation and makes it possible to engage predetermined targets during darkness or periods of reduced visibility.

Trigger Manipulation

- Pull the trigger to the rear and then release (not squeezed, see the above cycle of function). The weapon can be damaged by not pulling the trigger to the rear quickly and releasing it quickly when firing.

- Bursts of less than 6 rounds should not be fired.

- The rapid rate of fire of 200 rounds per minute is delivered in bursts of 10- to 12- rounds, which are fired 2 to 3 seconds apart.

- The sustained rate of fire of 100 rounds per minute is delivered in bursts of 6 to 8 rounds, which are fired 4 to 5 seconds apart.

Blank Firing Adapter

The Blank Firing Adapter (BFA) replaces the flash suppressor to allow for the firing of blanks in training exercises. This item is available from www.vig-sec.com

Installing the blank firing adapter-

1. To install the blank firing adapter, ensure the weapon has been properly cleared.

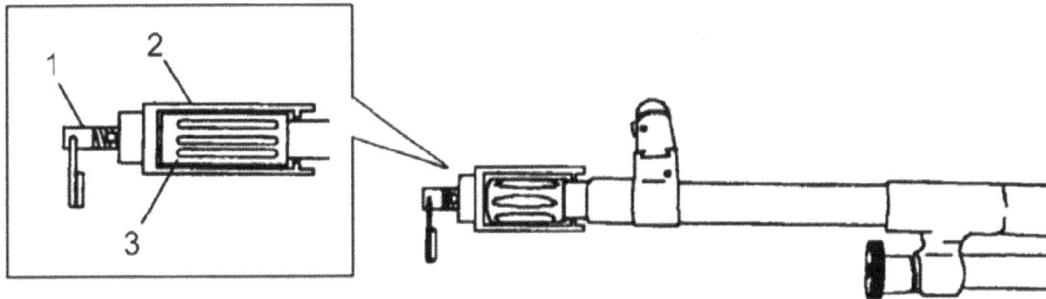

Figure 3-15 Blank firing adapter installation

2. Unscrew the shaft until it slides all the way to the rear. Install the chamber device over the flash suppressor and slide the shaft into the throat of the flash suppressor (Figure 3-15).

3. Then screw (regular threaded, right-turn direction) the shaft on the body of the chamber device until it is hand tight (Figure 3-15).

Removing the blank firing adapter-

1. To remove the blank firing adapter, ensure the weapon has been properly cleared.

2. Hold the barrel and rotate the chamber of the body about 180 degrees counterclockwise to break any carbon sealed between the shaft and the suppressor.

3. Unscrew the shaft until the threads disengage. Remove the chamber device from the suppressor.

Care of the MG While Using the BFA- A buildup of carbon inside the weapon causes friction between the moving parts. Carbon deposits build up rapidly when blanks are fired. When these deposits become excessive, stoppages occur. Therefore, the weapon must be kept clean, especially the gas system and chamber, during blank firing. To get the best performance with the BFA, the operator will perform the following:
   • Inspect the weapon for damaged parts, excessive wear, cleanliness, and proper lubrication before firing.

- When feasible, test fire the weapon using ball ammunition before attaching the BFA.
- Adjust the BFA to fit the weapon.
- Apply immediate action when stoppages occur.
- Clean the weapon including barrel assembly, gas cylinder, gas piston, gas port, chamber bore, and BFA.
- Clean and lubricate the entire weapon after firing 400 blank rounds.

Barrel Change Procedure

Changing the barrels will prolong the life of the barrel and equalize barrel wear.

Figure 3-16a carrying handle to right of weapon, depress the barrel-locking latch.

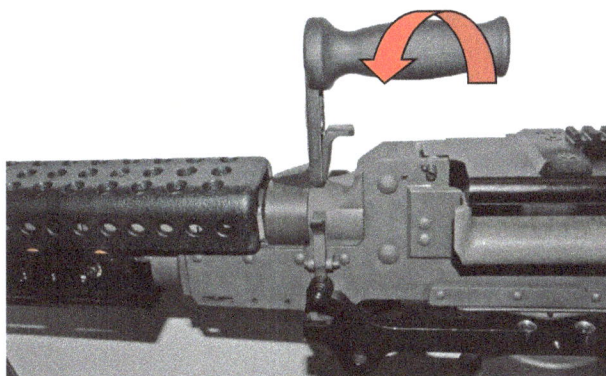

Figure 3-16b Rotate the carrying handle to the upright position (do not lift up on the barrel release).

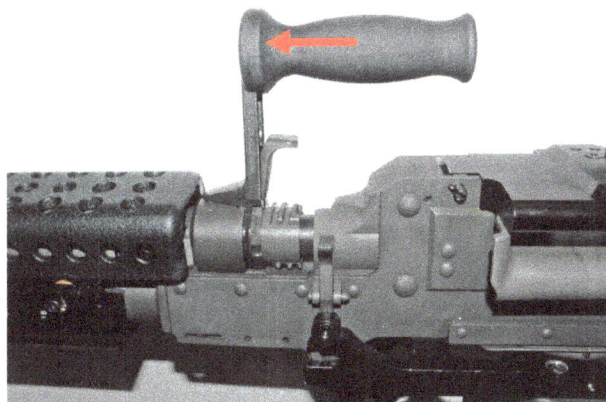

Figure 3-16c Push forward and up to remove the barrel from the receiver.

Unlocking and removing the barrel sequence

Inserting the new barrel-

Figure 3-17

Keeping the gun upright, pull the barrel to the rear, ensuring the gas regulator is guided into the gas cylinder (Figure 3-17). Pull the barrel fully into the receiver and rotate the carrying handle completely to the right, making sure to count the number of clicks. If the number of clicks falls between 2 to 7, the headspace is set correctly. If the number falls outside 2 to 7, turn it in to the unit armor (make sure that the threads on the barrel are located on top and bottom, and on the inside of the receiver, make sure that the threads are located on the left and right).

Gas setting

The M240 Series weapon has only one gas setting and is not adjustable. On MAG58 versions, the rate of fire may be controlled by three different settings. The first setting allows the weapon to cycle at 750 rounds per minute. The two remaining settings increase the rate of fire by 100 rounds/min per setting, the second setting being 850 rounds/min and third setting, 950 rounds per minute). These settings are changed by turning the gas regulator using the C-tool provided. It is generally performed before missions, as changing the setting is distracting at best under field or combat conditions. In event of sluggish operation due to fouling, the gas regulator is usually turned two positions up to provide more gas for reliable operation. This operation is usually done by the assistant operator, on instruction by the operator.

Sights/Zeroing the MAG58/M240

Figure 3-18 Photo of standard rear sight

Figure 3-19 Photo of standard front sight

Figure 3-20 Proper sight alignment of the front and rear sights

This section provides information on how to make corrections if the initial setting is not accurate. At a 10-meter target, each pastie is 1 cm square. Therefore, 10 clicks on the adjusting screw (windage) of the front-sight assembly in either direction moves the strike of the round left or right 1 cm. One complete turn on the front sight blade moves the strike of the round up or down 1 cm.

Elevation Correction- If the shot group is above or below the point of aim, the front sight posts must be adjusted using the front sight-adjusting tool. Unlock the front-sight retaining strap and rotate it up (Figures 3-21a and 3-21b).

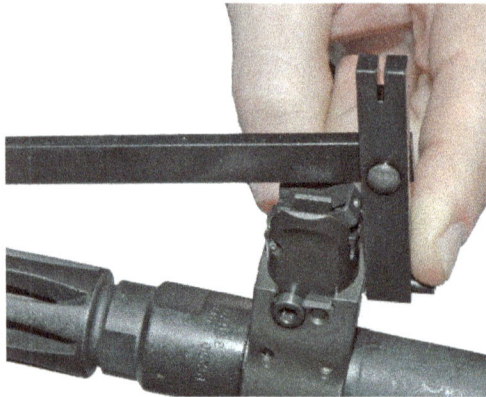

Figure 3-21a   **Figure 3-21b**
Unlocking for front sight prior to adjusting

If the shot group is above the point of aim, rotate the sight post counterclockwise. If the shot group is below the point of aim, rotate the sight post clockwise. Rotating the front sight post counterclockwise brings the point of impact down on the target. Rotating the front sight post clockwise brings the point of impact up on the target (Figure 3-22).

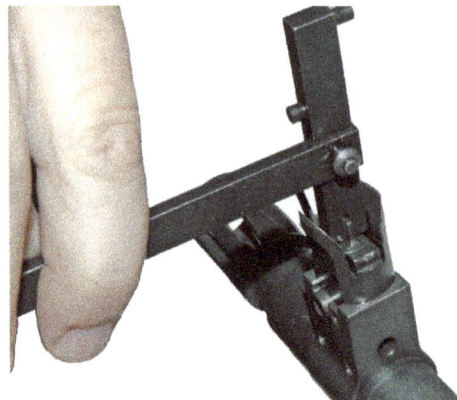

Figure 3-22 Adjusting for elevation change

At a range of 10 meters, one-half turn of the front sight post blade will move the point of impact by 5 mm or .5 cm. One full turn of the front sight post blade moves the point of impact by 1 cm. After rotating the front sight post blade the desired amount, lower the retaining strap, but do not lock it down until elevation is confirmed. If the front sight post blade must be rotated counterclockwise to a point where its base is past flush (Number 2 blade), it should be replaced with a Number 1 front sight blade, which is smaller than a Number 2 blade. If the front sight post blade must be rotated counterclockwise to a point where its base is more than one full turn past flush (Number 1 blade), it should be replaced with a Number 2 front sight blade, which is taller than a Number 1 blade.

Windage Correction- If the shot group is to the left of the point aim, move the front sight assembly to the right to shift the point of impact to the left (towards the point of aim). Using the front sight-adjusting tool, loosen (turn counterclockwise) the adjusting screw on the front-sight assembly the desired amount. Then tighten (turn clockwise) the opposite side screw on the left exactly the same number of clicks (Figure 3-23).

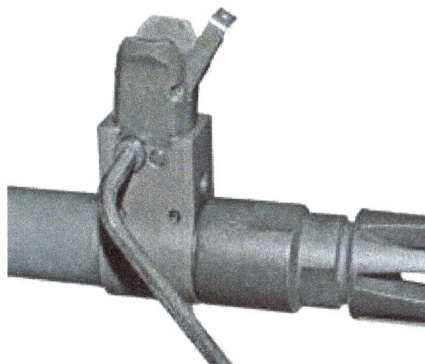

Figure 3-23 Adjusting for windage change

At a range of 10 meters, one complete rotation of the adjusting screws will move the point of impact 8 mm or .8 cm. As the adjusting screws are turned, noticeable clicks (eight per revolution) should be detected. Each click is 1 mm or .1 cm. If this is not the case, have your armorer repair it. The front sight windage-adjusting procedure is the combination of creating slack on one side, and then taking up that slack from the opposite side. The front sight-protector assembly should always be clamped between the heads of the two opposing screws. Remember, each time one screw is loosened or backed off, the opposite screw must be turned exactly the same amount. Check for play in the front-sight assembly by lightly clamping it between finger and thumb and attempting to move the sight assembly laterally. If you feel no play, the windage adjustment is completed. If evident, carefully check both screws for looseness (Figure 3-24).

Figure 3-24 Locking for front sight after adjusting

10-Meter Zeroing (Mechanical Zero)- Ten-meter zero (mechanical zero) is the standardized starting point for all weapons in the United States Army. The operator places the range scale on a range of 500 meters on the rear sight. He gets the front sight post blade approximately centered for both elevation and windage. The operator identifies what number blade is on the weapon for elevation.

1. Number 1 blade (low 9.8mm). Unlock the retaining strap and unscrew (counterclockwise) until the base of the blade is flush with the front sight-protector surface, and then make one full turn (counterclockwise). This should put the base of the blade past the base of the protector. Screw in (clockwise); counting the number of turns it takes until it stops, make sure the blade is on line with the barrel. If needed, back off until the blade is on line. Unscrew (counterclockwise) half the number of turns, which brings the blade to about the center.

2. Number 2 blade (high 11.8mm). Unlock the retaining strap and unscrew (counterclockwise) until the base of the blade is flush with the front sight-protector surface. Screw in (clockwise), counting the number of turns it takes until it stops. Making sure the blade is on line with the barrel. If needed, back off until the blade is on line. Unscrew (counterclockwise) half the number of turns. This procedure brings the blade to about the center. Assume the prone position and sight on the target. Ensure windage is accomplished by making sure the front sight protector is centered left and right on its base.

100 meters—one full turn moves strike 10.8 cm (4.25 inches)

200 meters—one full turn moves strike 21.6 cm (8.5 inches)

300 meters—one full turn moves strike 32.4 cm (12.75 inches)

400 meters—one full turn moves strike 43.2 cm (17 inches)

500 meters—one full turn moves strike 54 cm (21.25 inches)

600 meters—one full turn moves strike 64.8 cm (25.5 inches)

700 meters—one full turn moves strike 75.6 cm (29.75 inches)

800 meters—one full turn moves strike 86.4 cm (34 inches)

900 meters—one full turn moves strike 97.2 cm (38.25 inches)

Elevation Correction Chart for the M240B

100 meters—one full turn moves strike 8 cm (3.15 inches).

200 meters—one full turn moves strike 16 cm (6.3 inches).

300 meters—one full turn moves strike 24 cm (9.45 inches).

400 meters—one full turn moves strike 32 cm (12.6 inches).

500 meters—one full turn moves strike 40 cm (15.75 inches).

600 meters—one full turn moves strike 48 cm (18.9 inches).

700 meters—one full turn moves strike 56 cm (22 inches).

800 meters—one full turn moves strike 64 cm (25.2 inches).

900 meters—one full turn moves strike 72 cm (28.35 inches).

Windage Correction Chart for the M240B

Bipod Operations

The bipod assembly is used to fire from the prone position. The buttstock, in conjunction with the operator's non-firing hand, provides support for the weapon when firing in the bipod mode. The gas cylinder holds the bipod in place.

1. To lower the bipod legs, depress the bipod retaining latch while holding the bipod legs together to disengage from slots in the receiver. Then rotate the bipod legs down and release them so they lock in the vertical position. The bipod legs of the M240B do not extend (Figure 3-25).

2. To return the bipod to the locked, upright position, hold the bipod legs together to disengage them from the locked vertical position. Rotate the bipod legs rearward, depressing the bipod retaining latch, and engage the bipod leg hooks into the slots of the receiver. The bipod retaining latch will return to its original position, locking the bipod legs into position.

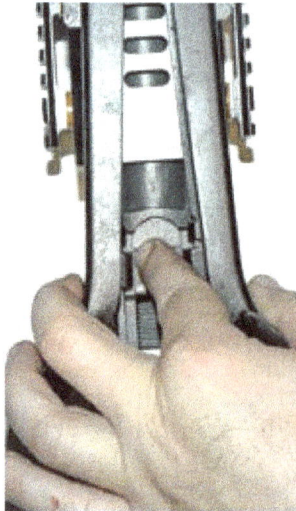

Figure 3-25 Lowering the bipod

Firing from the Bipod

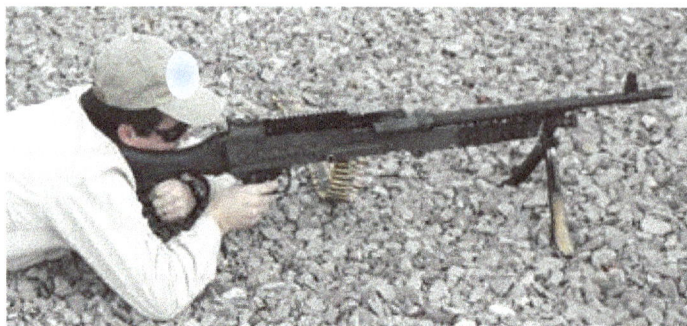

Figure 3-26 Firing from the bipod

• The rear sight is adjusted to the desired range of target.

- Assume a prone position behind the gun, with the right shoulder into the weapon, Figure 3-26.

- The right hand grasps the pistol grip and manipulates the trigger, Figure 3-26.

- Place the left hand on the comb of the stock, palm down or up, with the cheek resting lightly against the cover and/or the left hand, Figure 3-26.

- Both hands apply a firm steady pressure to the rear during aiming and firing.

- The bipod is not stable like a tripod; the body may move.

- When changing direction for minor adjustments, shift the shoulders and torso slightly.

- When changing direction for major adjustments, the entire body must be moved.

- Changing elevation is done by moving the elbows further apart or closer together.

Bipod Firing Positions -

Figure 3-27 Prone bipod position

Figure 3-28 Standing supported position (bipods are pushed against wall/structure)

Tripod Operations

M122A1 TRIPOD

The M122A1 tripod provides a stable mount for the MAG58/M240, and it permits a high degree of accuracy and control. The operator unfolds the front leg and positions it toward the target and spreads the rear legs until the leg lock engages.

The M122A1 tripod provides a stable mount for the MAG58/M240, and it permits a higher degree of accuracy and control. The tripod is recommended for marksmanship training and defensive employment. The M122A1 tripod consists of the tripod and flex-mount with T&E mechanism.

Mounting the MAG58/M240 on the Tripod- The tripod assembly provides a stable and relatively lightweight base that is far superior to the bipod. The tripod may be extended and collapsed without difficulty. It consists of a tripod head, one front leg and two rear legs, and traversing bar. The traversing bar connects the two rear legs. It is hinged on one side and has a sleeve and sleeve latch on the other that allows the tripod to collapse to a closed position for carrying or storage, or to lock in an open, extended position for use.

The traversing bar also supports the T&E mechanism. The increments are numbered every 100 mils to 425 mils right of center. On the bar is a scale that measures direction in mils. It is graduated in 5-mil increments and numbered every 100 mils to 450 mils left of the center.

1. The T&E mechanism provides controlled manipulation and the ability to engage predetermined targets.
    (a) The traversing portion of the mechanism consists of the traversing handwheel and traversing slide-lock-lever. As the traversing handwheel is turned, the muzzle of the weapon turns to the left or right, depending on the direction it is turned. Each click of the traversing handwheel indicates a 1-mil change in direction of the muzzle: 1 click equals 1 mil. There is a total of 100-mils traverse (50 mils right and 50 mils left of center).

    (b) The elevating portion of the mechanism consists of the elevating handwheel. The elevating handwheel has a mil-click device built into it (1 click equals 1 mil). Engraved into the handwheel is a scale divided into 5-mil divisions and 1-mil subdivisions for a total of 50-mil increments. There are 200 mils above and 200 mils below the zero mark for a total of 400 mils in elevation change. Elevation readings are taken in two parts. First, the major reading is taken from the elevation screw plate. The second, minor reading is from the handwheel. The two readings are separated by a slash (/) when they are recorded.

    (c) The traversing slide-lock-lever allows rapid lateral adjustments along the traversing bar. Direction readings are taken from the scale on the traversing bar, using the left side of the traversing slide as an index. The direction of the reading comes from the position of the muzzle, not the position of the slide.

2. The flex-mount consists of the mount itself and the traversing and elevating mechanism. It joins the weapon and the T&E mechanism to the tripod. The flex-mount enhances the stability of the tripod platform and dampens the recoil of the weapon.

3. To setup the tripod, the operator unfolds the front leg and spreads the rear legs until the leg lock engages (Figure 3-29).

Figure 3-29 M122A1 tripod extended

1 – Sleeve Lock   5 – Tripod Head
2 – Sleeve   6 – Front Leg
3 – Rear Legs   7 – Pintle Lock
4 – Traversing Bar   8 – Pintle

4. Prepare the T&E mechanism for mounting. First center the elevating and traversing handwheel. To do this, rotate the elevation handwheel until about 1 1/2 inches (two fingers) are visible on the upper elevating screw; rotate the traversing slide until approximately two fingers are visible on the lower elevating screw. The operator rotates the traversing handwheel towards his body as far as it will go, and then he turns it away two complete revolutions. He checks the traversing handwheel scale to ensure the "0" on the scale is aligned with the "0" index line before and after the two revolutions. The T&E should be centered now (Figure 3-30).

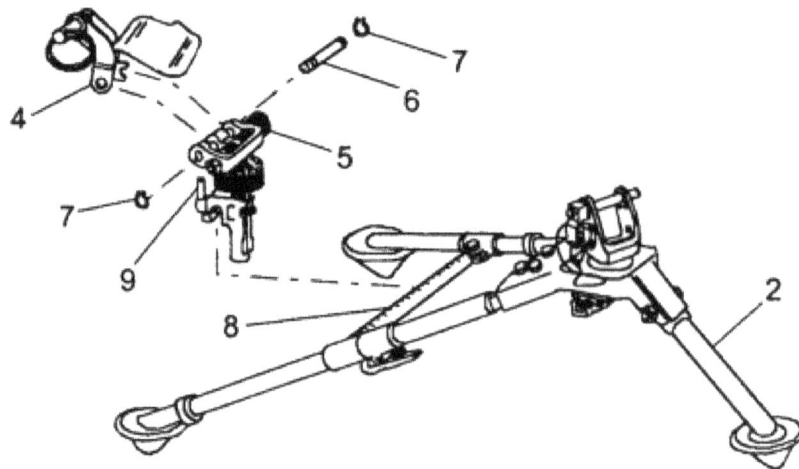

Figure 3-30

5. Mount the T&E mechanism, pintle assembly, and fork assembly to the M122A1 tripod. With the T&E roughly centered, place the pintle assembly (1) into the sleeve bushing on the tripod leg assembly (2). Release the pintle lock (3) on the tripod leg assembly to secure the pintle assembly to the tripod (Figure 3-30).

NOTE: The deflector on the fork assembly should deflect to the right.

6. Align the holes in the fork assembly (4) with the holes in the T&E (5). Insert the pin (6) through the fork assembly and the T&E and secure with "C" clamps.

7. Mount the weapon on the M122A1 tripod assembly (Figure 3-31). Tilt the muzzle down slightly and insert the weapon's front receiver bushing (1) into the slots in the pintle assembly (2). Insert the quick-release pin (3) through the pintle (2) and front receiver bushing (1). Place the T&E assembly (5) (with fork assembly attached) onto the traverse bar (8) of the tripod leg assembly (2). Lock the T&E mechanism into place by turning the lock lever (9) clockwise. Lower the rear of the weapon into the fork assembly (4). Align the mounting holes (5) in the trigger housing with the hole in the fork assembly (4). Insert the spring pin (6) through the holes in the trigger assembly and fork, but make sure the weapon is securely attached.

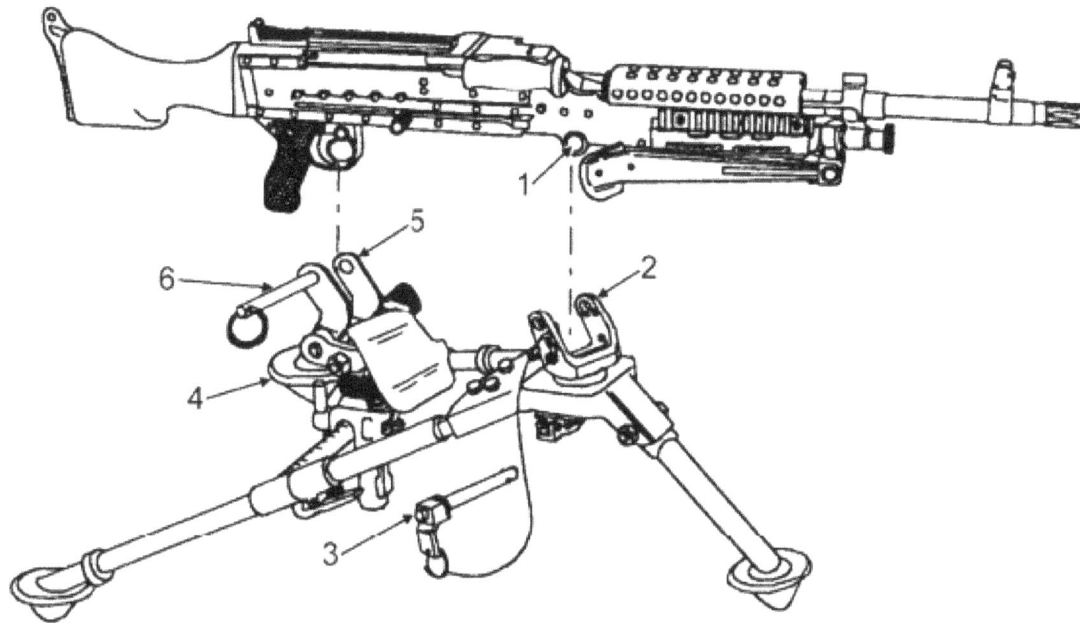

Figure 3-31 Mounting the M240B on the M122A1

Dismounting the M240B from the M122A1 Tripod- Dismount the MAG58/M240 from the M122A1 tripod by first removing the spring pin from the fork assembly and then disengage the quick-release pin from the pintle and the front receiver bushing. Now, raise the weapon up and off the tripod assembly.

Medium Machine Gun Tripod (Lightweight) [MMGT(LW)]

Figure 3-32 Tripod collapsed in storage/movement configuration

Figure 3-33 Tripod extended in compact configuration

Figure 3-34 Tripod fully extended configuration

The MMGT(LW) is a lightweight (5 pounds), man-packable, weapon mount and control that provides an accurate and repeatable means to aim and shift the fire of the M240G Medium Machine Gun (MMG). The MMGT(LW) consists of a tripod and a Traverse and Elevation (T&E) control mechanism, Figures 3-32, 3-33, & 3-34.

The MMGT(LW) will be used with the M240G MMG in all ground-mount applications. It is a direct replacement for the M122 Tripod System (the tripod and T&E mechanism currently used with the M60E3 MMG). The MMGT(LW) will enhance the capability of the Marine Corps three-man MMG team by providing them a lightweight means to engage targets accurately with the M240G MMG.

Proper Body Position to Fire

The Operator's Position - The operator assumes the prone position behind the gun in the same manner as with a bipod-mounted gun. The difference is with the left hand. The skeletonized buttstock is grasped with the left hand, palm down, and a firm rearward pressure is exerted with both hands. Exert pressure with the right shoulder. Rest the cheek lightly on the buttstock of the gun while aiming and firing.

The Team Leader's/Assistant Operator Position - This position is the same for both bipod- and tripod-mounted guns. Assume a prone position on the right side of the gun, ensuring that head and eyes are even with the feed way. Load, unload, and change barrels from this position.

Firing

Point the muzzle of the gun in the general direction of the target by releasing the traversing lock. Secure the lock lever when on target.

Place the estimated range on the rear sight, and manipulate the gun until there is a proper sight picture.

Unlike the bipod, the tripod provides a stable base and controlled manipulation, making the use of the sight redundant.

Manipulation - All manipulation is accomplished by loosening the two hand levers with the left hand. If both direction and elevation changes are required to engage a target, manipulate direction first, then elevation.

To traverse, place the left hand on the traversing hand lever, thumb up. To move the muzzle to the right, the operator pushes away with the thumb: PUSH RIGHT. To move the muzzle to the left, the operator pulls to the rear with the thumb: PULL LEFT.

To search, rest the left hand on the elevating hand lever. To move the muzzle up, the operator pushes away with the thumb: PUSH UP. To move the muzzle down, the operator pulls to the rear with the thumb: PULL DOWN.

Other MAG58/M240 firing positions

Figure 3-35 Prone tripod position

Figure 3-36 Seated tripod position

Figure 3-37 Anti-aircraft/High-angle tripod position

Figure 3-38 Kneeling assistant gunner-supported position

Vehicle Mount

MAG58/M240 Vehicle Mount available from www.vig-sec.com. This mount is a custom-made high-quality mount to allow the operator to mount a MAG58/M240 to all US military pintle mounts, whether a US tripod, ring mount, or pedestal mount that is also available.

In addition to the mounts described above, there exists a flexible vehicle mount, which accepts a standard MAG58/M240.

MK93 Mount

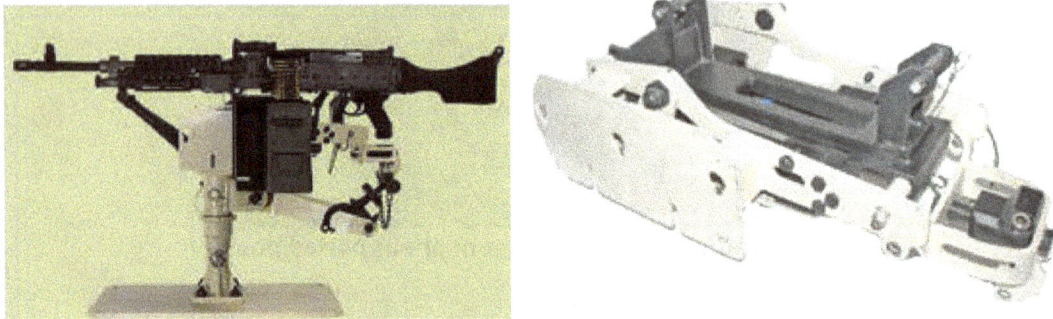

Figure 3-39 MAG58/M240 vehicle mount and cradle

This MK93 Machine Gun Mount is a new (2004) stronger design by the U.S. Army. The mount accepts the M2HB 12.7mm machine gun and the MK19 40mm machine gun and is adapted to the M240 and is designed for use on HMMWVs, trucks, and armored vehicles. With its small pintle, it fits into a variety of tripods, pedestals, and the Universal Pintle Adapter (UPA). The left rail supports an interface plate that accepts a variety of quick-removable ammo-can holders. The M2HB weapon is held in place by front and rear stainless-steel ball-lock pins. A slider system with two hydraulic shock absorbers reduces firing shock in both recoil and counter recoil for the M2HB. The normal recoil of 1200 pounds is reduced to under 500 pounds peak.

An optional Adapter Kit (M35-800) manufactured by Military Systems Group provides for installation of the M240 or the M249 weapons. It is not recommended to use this Machine Gun Mount with the Swing Arm system or in Naval applications due to its fabrication using carbon steel.

Mounting the M240 on the MK93 Mount

Figure 3-40 MK 93 in M2 BMG configuration

Figure 3-41 Rotating the platforms on the cylinders in and down and turn the rear locking point (slide forward and rotate, and then return to the rear)

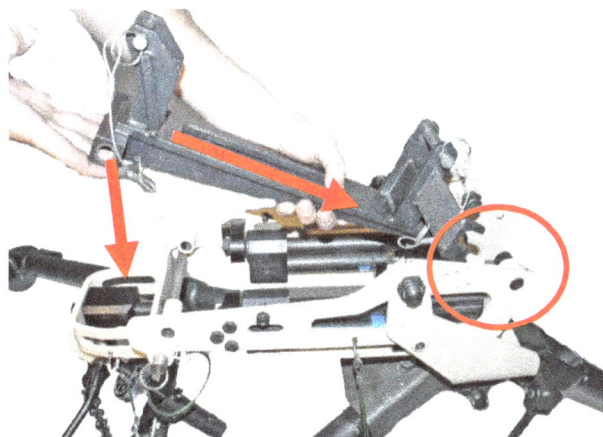

Figure 3-42 Placing the forks of the M240 adapter onto the front lugs (used for mounting Mk 19)

Figure 3-43 Inserting rear locking pin and pull pins in the adapter to receive the MG

Figure 3-44 Inserting the front mounting pin (bipods must be out of storage position)

Figure 3-45 Inserting the rear mounting pin

Section 4

Performance Problems

Malfunction and Immediate Action Procedures-

A malfunction is a failure of the weapon to function properly. Defective ammunition or improper operation of the weapon by an operator is not considered a malfunction of the weapon. Some of the more common malfunctions of the MAG58/M240 are sluggish operation and/or a runaway weapon.

Sluggish operation and the corrective action- Sluggish operation (gun fires very slowly) of the weapon is usually due to excessive friction caused by dirt or carbon, lack of proper lubrication, burred parts, or excessive loss of gas. Move the gas regulator setting to the number two or three position and re-test until the weapon functions properly. If this step does not correct the sluggish operation, then disassemble, clean, and lubricate the weapon while inspecting the parts for burrs or damage. Replace parts as necessary.

Runaway weapon and corrective action- A runaway weapon is a weapon that continues to fire after the trigger has been released. It may be induced by a worn sear, worn sear notch, or short recoil, i.e., the operating group recoils to feed and fire but not sufficiently enough for the sear to engage the sear notch. Short recoil may be caused by loss of gas or excessive carbon buildup in the operating rod tube. To correct this condition, hold the weapon on target until the ammunition belt is expended. Disassemble the weapon and check the gas port plug and gas cylinder extension, and clean the operating rod. Replace parts as necessary and re-test.

Stoppages- A stoppage is an interruption in the cycle of operation caused by a faulty gun or ammunition. In short, the gun stops firing. A stoppage must be cleared quickly by applying immediate action.

Immediate Action- This is the prompt action taken by the operator to reduce a stoppage of the machine gun without investigating the cause. If the gun stops firing, the operator performs immediate action. Hang fire and cook off are two terms that describe ammunition condition and should be understood in conjunction with immediate action procedures.
- Wait 5 seconds.
- Within next 5 seconds, pull and lock the cocking handle to the rear and observe ejection port.
- If round or cartridge is ejected, take aim and attempt to fire.
- If no rounds are ejected, or if it does not fire, take remedial action.

Remedial Action-

1. COLD WEAPON: Less than 200 rounds in 2 minutes.
    a. Pull the cocking handle to the rear locking the bolt if not done already.
    b. Place weapon on "SAFE" if not done already.
    c. Place the weapon on the ground away from the face and open feed cover.
    d. Remove stuck or ruptured cartridge.

2. HOT WEAPON: 200 rounds or more in 2 minutes or less.
    a. Place the weapon on "SAFE".
    b. Let weapon cool for 15 minutes.
    c. Follow procedures as outlined above.

Hang Fire- Occurs when the cartridge primer has detonated after being struck by the firing pin, but some problem with the propellant powder causes it to burn too slowly, which delays the firing of the projectile. Time (5 seconds) is allotted for this malfunction before investigating a stoppage further because of potential injury to personnel and damage to equipment.

Cook Off- Occurs when the heat of the weapon is high enough to cause the propellant powder inside the round to ignite even though the primer has not been struck. Immediate action is to unload the weapon immediately and allow it cool prior to reloading and firing.

Misfire Procedures

Immediate Action- This action is performed when the operator has a failure to fire, which is when the trigger is pulled, the bolt moves forward, and the weapon does not fire. If a cartridge case, belt link, or a round is ejected, push the cocking handle to its forward position, take aim on the target, and pull the trigger. If the weapon does not fire, take remedial action. If a cartridge case, belt link, or a round is not ejected, take remedial action.

Remedial Action- When immediate action fails to reduce the stoppage, remedial action must be taken. Prior to investigating the cause of the stoppage, you must clear the weapon, and this step may involve some disassembly of the weapon and replacement of parts to correct the problem.

Remedial actions for stoppages are as follows.

Stuck Cartridge- Some swelling of the cartridge occurs when it fires. If the swelling is excessive, the cartridge will be fixed tightly in the chamber. If the extractor spring has weakened and does not tightly grip the base of the cartridge, it may fail to extract a round when the bolt moves to the rear.

1. Ensure the bolt is locked to the rear.
2. Place the weapon on "SAFE" and allow the gun to cool if it is a hot gun.
3. Insert a length of cleaning rod into the muzzle to push the round out through the chamber.

[WARNING] If nothing is ejected and the barrel is hot (200 rounds or more in 2 minutes or less), do not open the cover. Push the safety to the rear, which places the weapon on "SAFE". Keep the weapon pointed down range and remain clear for 15 minutes, and then clear the weapon.

Ruptured Cartridge - Sometimes a cartridge is in a weakened condition after firing. In addition, it may swell as described above. In this case, a properly functioning extractor may sometimes tear the base of the cartridge off as the bolt moves to the rear, leaving the rest of the cartridge wedged inside the chamber. The ruptured cartridge extractor must be used in this instance to remove it.

Remove the barrel and insert the shell extractor into the chamber to grip and remove the remains of the cartridge.

The ruptured case extractor must be used if the empty cartridge case is ripped in half, leaving the front half of the casing in the chamber and preventing the next loaded round to seat in to the chamber. To extract this case neck, you must screw the extractor on the rod section and push it up into the chamber fully so you can pull the case neck out.

REFERENCES:
* *MCWP 3-15.1: Machine Guns and Machine Gun Gunnery*
* *FM 23-67 Crew-Served Machine Guns*

Appendix A - Ammunition

WARNING- Inspect all cartridges for uniformity, cleanliness, and serviceability. Check all for undented primers, and only use issued ammunition.

The 7.62x51mm (.308 Winchester) ammunition used by the MAG58/M240 is produced by most NATO countries and in many different countries. The 7.62x51mm cartridges will be encountered in both brass and steel cases; however, brass cases are more prolific. The 7.62mm is the diameter of the bullet, 51mm is the length of the case, and it is a rimless cartridge.

Originally created by the U.S. Army to replace the 30-06, the .308 Winchester (7.62x51mm in military form) ranks among the most versatile and popular centerfire cartridges in the world. The .308 serves police and military marksmen, Palma competitors, F-Class shooters, and deer-hunters equally well. The .308 delivers superb accuracy along with outstanding barrel life.

The following is a brief list of the different types of ammunition and their uses:

Figure A-1 Linked steel-core ammunition

- **7.62mm, NATO, Ball, M80**: 146-grain 7.62x51mm NATO ball cartridge. Steel-core ball - for use against light material targets, personnel, or training. The steel-core ball weighs 146 grains and has a muzzle velocity of 825 m/s (2700 fps). There are no tip markings on the bullet.

- **7.62mm, NATO, Tracer, M62**: 142-grain tracer cartridge, orange cartridge tip. Tracer - for observation of fire, incendiary effects, signaling, and use during training. Green-tipped marking denotes the green trace when fired. Maximum tracer burnout is 900 meters.

- **7.62mm, NATO, Armor-Piercing, M61**: 150.5-grain 7.62x51mm NATO armor-piercing round, black cartridge tip.

- **7.62mm, NATO, Blank, M82** - for use during training when simulating live fire. If blanks are to be fired from the MAG58/M240 machine gun, a blank adapter must first be fitted to the muzzle. Without the blank adapter, insufficient gas pressure is generated to cycle the weapon properly. Crimped purple nose.

- **7.62mm, NATO, Dummy, M63** - for use during training and armorer duty.

- **7.62mm, NATO, Tracer, M276**: 7.62x51mm NATO so-called "Dim Tracer" with reduced effect primarily for use with night vision devices. Green cartridge tip with pink ring.

- **7.62mm, NATO, M948**: 7.62x51mm NATO Saboted Light Armor-Piercing cartridge.

- **7.62mm, NATO, Armor-Piercing, M993**: 126.6-grain 7.62x51mm NATO armor-piercing round, black cartridge tip. Armor piercing - for use against lightly armored targets where armor-piercing effects are desired.

M13 Link

Ammunition for use in machine guns is issued in metallic link belts. The 7.62mm M13 links are manufactured with partially open loops and have a positioning finger on one side which snaps into extractor grooves of the cartridge to retain the cartridge in proper feed alignment. This link design permits a portion of bolt to ride through link loop openings and push cartridges forward and out of the link into chamber for firing. Weapons using this type link are designed and manufactured with a short receiver.

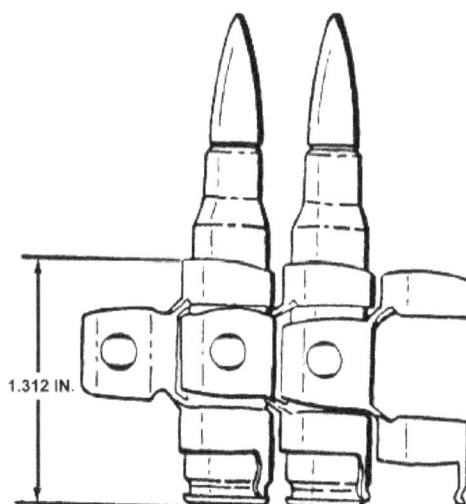

1.312 IN.

Figure A-2 M13 Link

Storage- Ammunition is stored under cover. If ammunition is in the open, it must be kept at least 6 inches above the ground and covered with a double thickness of tarpaulin. The cover must be placed so that it protects the ammunition, yet allows ventilation. Trenches are dug to divert water from flowing under the ammunition.

Ammunition precautions

A. Ammunition containers should not be opened until you are ready to use them.

B. You should protect the ammunition from mud, dirt, and water. If the ammunition gets dirty or corroded, it must be cleaned before firing.

C. Do not expose ammunition to the direct rays of the sun for long periods of time.

D. Do not oil or grease ammunition, as it will collect dirt.

E. Replace any defective ammunition when you check it prior to firing.

F. Any ammunition marked **"FOR TRAINING PURPOSE ONLY"** is not to be fired over the heads of friendly troops.

Care, Handling, and Preservation- Ammunition should not be removed from the airtight containers until ready for use. Ammunition removed from the airtight containers, particularly in damp climates, may corrode.
- Ammunition must be protected from mud, dirt, and moisture. If it gets wet or dirty, the ammunition must be wiped off before using. Lightly corroded cartridges are wiped off as soon as the corrosion is discovered. Heavily corroded, dented, or loose projectiles should not be fired.
- Ammunition must be protected from the direct rays of the sun. Excessive pressure from the heat may cause premature detonation.
- Oil should never be used on ammunition. Oil collects dust and other abrasives that may possibly damage the operating parts of the weapon.

Packaging- The ammunition box contains two cartons. Each carton has a bandoleer for carrying purposes. Each carton contains 100 rounds and weighs about 7 pounds. Ammunition in the bandoleers may be linked together, attached to the hanger assembly, and fired from the container, or the bandoleers may be removed for firing.

NATO 7.62 AMMO
4-1 COMBAT MIX

BLACK

RED OR
ORANGE

ARMOR
PIERCING

BALL

TRACER

DUMMY

IMPROVED
BLANK

M61/M993

M80

M62

M172

M82

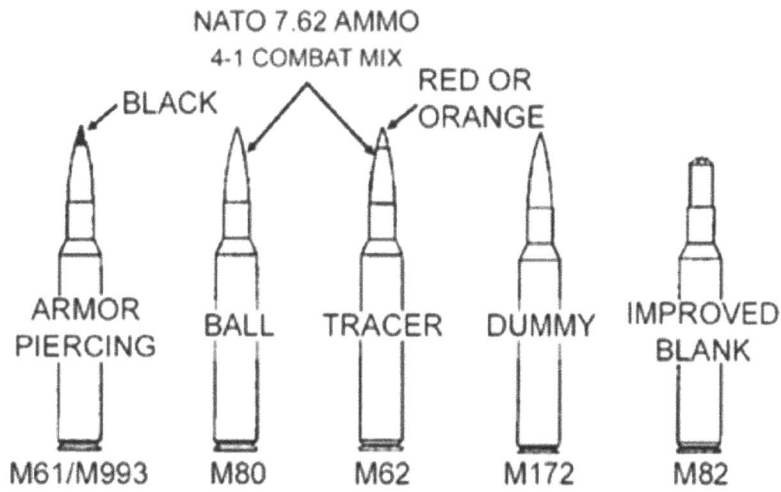

Figure A-3 Various ammunition examples

7.62x51mm Ballistic Chart

M80 7.62x51mm NATO

BC: 0.408 G1   CAL: 0.308 in   WGT: 150 gr

MV: 2820 ft/s   CH: 10 ft

WS: 10 mph   TS: 10 mph

T: 59 °F   PC: 29.92 in Hg   H: 0%   A: 0 ft

SH: 1.5 in   SO: 0 in   ZH: 0 in   LOS: 0°

Range	Drop		Wind (10 mph)		Lead (10 mph)	
(m)	(in)	(in)	(in)	(in)	(in)	(in)
100	-0.0	-0.0	1.0	1.0	21.4	21.4
200	-4.8	-4.8	4.0	4.0	44.9	44.9
300	-17.1	-17.1	9.5	9.5	70.7	70.7
350	-26.6	-26.6	13.2	13.2	84.7	84.7
400	-38.7	-38.7	17.7	17.7	99.4	99.4
500	-71.7	-71.7	29.1	29.1	131.2	131.2
600	-118.9	-118.9	44.2	44.2	166.8	166.8
700	-183.7	-183.7	63.5	63.5	206.5	206.5
800	-270.4	-270.4	87.3	87.3	250.7	250.7
900	-384.2	-384.2	115.8	115.8	299.6	299.6
1000	-530.6	-530.6	148.5	148.5	352.7	352.7
1100	-714.6	-714.6	184.8	184.8	409.4	409.4
1200	-941.1	-941.1	224.4	224.4	469.4	469.4

7.62x51mm Ballistic Chart

NOTE: Minute of Angle (MOA): The term Minute of Angle, referred to as MOA, is actually a unit of measure dealing with circles found in surveying, navigation, and mathematics. One Minute of Angle is 1/60th of one degree of a circle. A circle has 360 degrees, and 21,600 Minutes of Angle are in a circle.

If you were to look at a circle that has a radius of 100 yards and project lines out from the center in Minute of Angle increments, you would find that at 100 yards away from the center of the circle, the distance between the Minute of Angle lines would be 1.0472 inches.

Over time, one Minute of Angle at 100 yards has been rounded off to one inch and has become a standard unit of measurement for bullet trajectory calculations, comparisons, accuracy levels, and the sighting-in of firearms.

The chart below illustrates the Minute of Angle concept and plots what one, two, and three Minutes of Angle would be at various distances.

One, Two and Three Minute of Angle (MOA) Chart

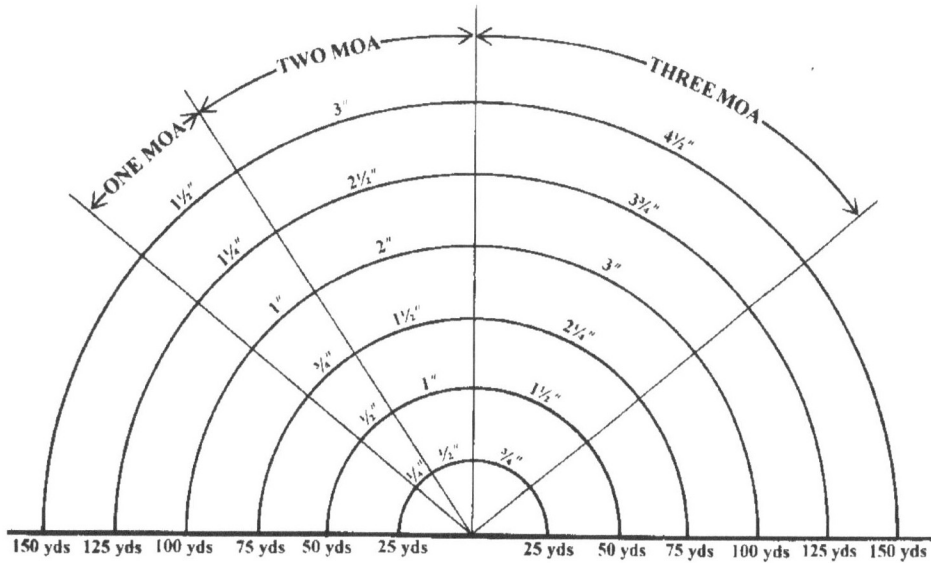

The chart below shows another viewpoint of how Minute of Angle measurements apply to firearms and accuracy. Frequently, a weapon's accuracy is described as being able to fire groups that are less than one Minute of Angle at 100 yards. This description would mean that if the shooter fired five rounds at a target 100 yards away and used correct sight alignment, the group would measure less than one inch.

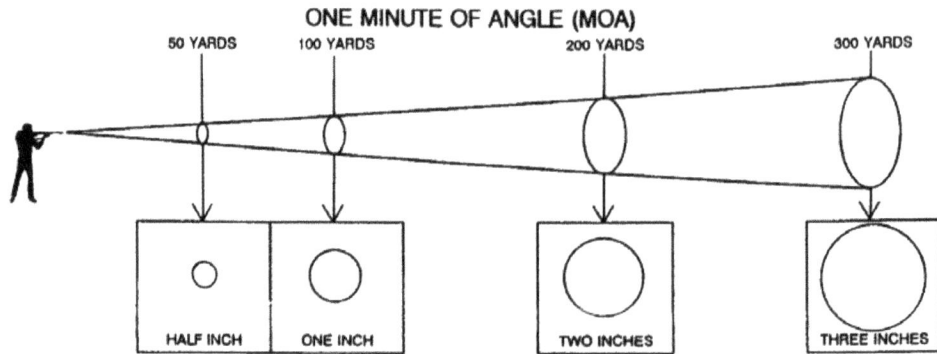

ONE MINUTE OF ANGLE (MOA)

MAG58/M240 Ammunition Containers and Links

The weapon is fed by non-disintegrating metal link belts. Current belts are joined 25-round sections. Link containers hold the ammunition belts securely to the bottom of the weapon or onto the tripod include:

Figure A-4 50-round soft ammo carriers

- 50-round soft nylon

AMMUNITION ADAPTER -The ammunition adapter is used on the M240B machine gun when firing. This adapter allows the operator to use the 100-round carton and bandoleer. (Figure A-5)

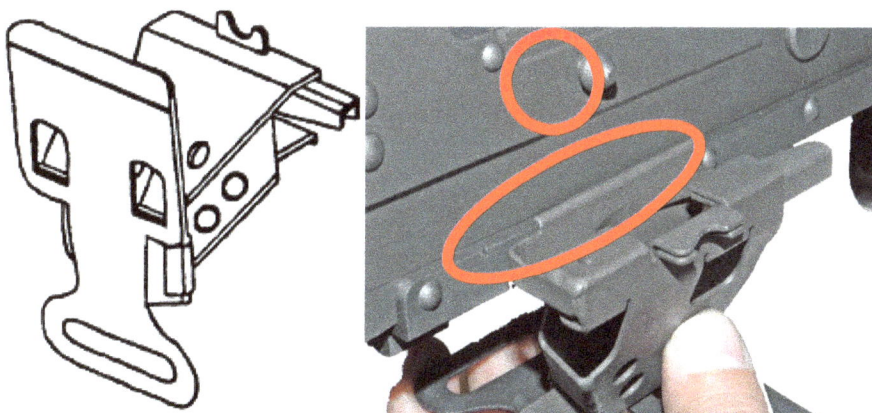

Figure A-5 Ammunition adapter – set the flat base in the groove and pivot up

Attaching the Ammunition Adapter- The ammunition adapter is fitted to the left side and under the feed tray of the receiver. When looking at the left side of the receiver, you will see a slot and a button under the feed tray (Figure A-5). First attach the bandoleer holder to the base of the adapter by inserting the tapered end (green plastic) of the holder into the adapter. Open the cover assembly and raise the feed tray. Insert the curved lip of the adapter assembly into the slot located in the rail on the left of the receiver, below the feed tray, depressing the lever on the adapter assembly and pushing the assembly towards the receiver until it is against the receiver (Figure A-6). Release the lever to allow the adapter assembly to secure itself onto the button on the receiver.

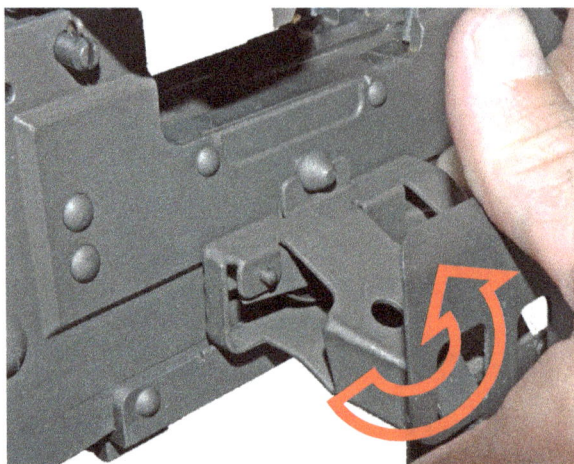

Figure A-6 lock the carrier into the button

Care of the Ammunition Adapter- Over a prolonged period, the moving parts, to include plastic, will start to wear out and break.
- Inspect the adapter for damaged parts, excessive wear, and cleanliness whenever the weapon is taken out of the arms room.
- When feasible, test-fit the adapter.
- After using the adapter, inspect to ensure it is still operational.

Typical packaging is four 100-round cardboard boxes in a cotton bandoleer in a sealed metal can, with two metal cans in a wooden case for a total of 800 rounds. The individual rounds will be packaged in paper in quantities of 20 rounds.

Appendix B- Ammunition Comparison

9x18mm Makarov · 9x19mm Luger · 7.62x25mm Tokarev · .45 ACP

Pistols and Submachine Guns

NATO & SOVIET BLOC
AMMUNITION COMPARISON

5.56x 45mm · 5.45x 39mm · 5.56x 45mm · 7.62x 39mm · 7.62x 51mm · 7.62x 54R mm · 12.7x99mm (.50 BMG) · 12.7x108mm

Assault Rifles   Sniper Rifles and Machine Guns

www.ingramcontent.com/pod-product-compliance
Lightning Source LLC
Chambersburg PA
CBHW080525110426

42742CB00017B/3233